An Intuitive Life

A practical guide to living in harmony with your inner wisdom

Diana Hunter

National Library of Australia Cataloguing-in-Publication data:

ISBN-13: 978-0-6456298-0-4 (paperback edition)
ISBN-13: 978-0-6456298-1-1 (e book)

Cover Illustration Copyright © 2023
Cover design by Jo Edgar-Baker
Book design and production by Jo Edgar Baker
Author Portrait by Lauren Biggs Photography

Book Coach and Editing - Jennifer Marr
Additional Editing - Leigh Wilks

Dedication

To those
who bravely bring forward
a new dawn of love and compassion on Earth
intuitively remembering its healing power.

Acknowledgements

Thank you to those people who have touched my life
and contributed to my way of being.
It is with deep gratitude I acknowledge the
priceless guidance I have received over the years from:

Sharon Whiteman my mentor and friend.

My Women's Circle – who hold me in authenticity and
reflect my worth.

Lee Carroll and the works of Kryon[1] – my spiritual guide
and teacher, and whose teachings have taken me to a new
depth of understanding and connection with my intuition.

Yve Betar, Vince Betar; River and Diamond Jamieson[2] –
whose work set me on the track of deep emotional truth.

Esther Hicks and the works of Abraham[3] – for keeping my
mindset on track.

My sincere appreciation to all the wonderful women
who contributed their stories to this book for the
upliftment of others.

Table of Contents

Foreword 7

Purpose of this Guidebook 9

1. Intuition – A Gateway to Transform Your Life 11

2. Foundations for Intuitive Mastery 21

3. Your Emotions Are the Key 39

4. Going to the Heart of the Matter 59

5. Small Steps Lead to Leaps of Faith 81

6. The Voice of Your Intuition 99

7. What do You Want? 117

8. Intuition versus Fantasy 129

9. Your Relationship with Earth and Nature 147

10. Spiritual Assistance 167

11. Living an Intuitive Life 185

Recommended Resources 188

Endnotes 189

About the Author 190

Foreword

Is it possible that your intuition has guided you to choose this book and read these very words? If so, there is a clear invitation for you.

Are you open to discovering something new about yourself? Are you ready to explore the information within this book with an open heart and childlike wonder? Are you ready to deepen the connection with your innate wisdom so that you can live your life in a way that is filled with miraculous synchronicities?

All this and more is possible if you follow the path offered within *An Intuitive Life*.

Everyone has intuition, but not everyone has mastered the art of *listening* to their inner intuitive voice. One of the reasons why we tend to ignore our intuition is because it presents itself in a fleeting, elusive way. Sometimes it is even difficult to describe what our first intuitive thought was; much like a dream, it's something we can't explain. Another reason why it's difficult to follow our intuition is because our intuitive thoughts are often in direct opposition to what our intellect and logic are telling us. Yet, when we only follow our intellect and logic, we often miss opportunities and later realise we should have trusted that elusive, intuitive thought.

So, why is our intuition so elusive?

It's important to understand that intuition does not come from synaptic thought – the brain's thinking engine. Your brain is an amazing super-computer. It gives you past experiences that help you survive in future times. For example, if you touch a hot stove and burn your finger, chances are you are unlikely to ever do that again. This is because your brain gives you signals for life, every time you see a hot stove you think – danger! Do not touch the hot stove! All of these past experiences are amplified and applied in relationships, society, the workplace, and everything else.

So, your survival depends upon what your brain is telling you *is there*, or *not there*, to help you navigate reality. You rely on your past experience, transmitted to you via synaptic thought, to steer and guide you. Then suddenly you experience an intuitive thought that comes and goes so fast that you cannot be certain if it even happened! And you wonder, "*What was that?*"

Often, that intuitive flash was so fleeting that you are not even certain what the message was about. Your intuitive thought does not mirror your synaptic brain function, which is why it can be difficult to pin down or act upon. Yet, you know, there is something there!

How does one master the art of intuitive communication?

Thankfully, what you are about to read offers a practical guide on how you can enhance your natural ability to connect with your innate wisdom. You've already made the first step. You've decided to read this book. Congratulations on not only listening to your intuition, but for following up with action. You are well and truly on your way to creating a more purposeful and rewarding life. I'm so excited for you and am cheering you on from the sidelines.

Love and blessings

Monika Muranyi[4]

Kryon[5] Author and Spiritual Teacher

Purpose of this Guidebook

This is a comprehensive guide to the many facets of intuition and how to build a living relationship with your inner guidance system.

You will learn the foundational elements to recognise its voice and respond to its call. Practical methods and easy-to-follow steps are offered to develop your unique intuitive style. So, you can experience all aspects of life, from the simple to the more complex, in the flow of your innate wisdom.

Start anywhere

My suggestion is to focus on the information that most calls to you. That is, follow your intuition when reading or using this material. Sometimes you might find yourself drawn back to review certain sections of the book as your life unfolds. Intuitive development is not meant to be a linear process. Working with your intuition is a lifetime journey that will reward you with ease, joy and fulfilment along the way.

Build connection through practical steps

The practical steps at the end of each chapter are designed to move you into alignment with your inner knowing and open the channels to receiving your innate wisdom throughout your daily life, work, and relationships. These steps will also bring additional benefits to your personal fulfilment. They are designed to call benevolent energy into your life, so this becomes a natural part of your everyday experience.

I invite you to enjoy your journey of intuitive mastery.

With love,

Diana Hunter
Intuition Guide

Your intuition is guiding you
every step of the way
for purposeful life expansion.

1.

Intuition – A Gateway to Transform Your Life

Experience has shown me that backing my intuition with action can lead me through a learning curve as well as a level of personal development. I've also found that I may feel some resistance along the way. So, the path of following my intuition has often been a transformative process. This book project has certainly contained all of the above for me.

In fact, *An Intuitive Life* is the result of authentic, intuition-inspired writing.

Prior to receiving this inspiration, I had no desire or thought of writing a book. Yet, as someone committed to trusting and following my intuition over many decades, I began experiencing a strong recurring intuitive sense to put my insights into a guidebook. I felt moved to offer others direction in developing and enhancing the connection with their inner knowing. This repeated urge was unmistakeable, and I knew to take action.

With a deep sense of trust in that inner guidance, I simply began to write. I had no idea of the final outcome or how I was going to share it with others; I just knew I needed to start. Intuition can often be this way; it inspires us to action without a clear view of the possible reason or end result.

From my extensive, first-hand experience, I've learned the following:

1. **Intuition is your assistant navigator in life.** It is communication from a greater wisdom that you can access from within. It has many expressions, speaks in a variety of ways, and each person has their own individual repertoire. In fact, your intuition is like a dear friend, always on standby

to support you. Trusting your inner guidance is foundational in order to identify and follow your unique path in life. This intuitive path is one that will bring you the utmost fulfilment and happiness, one that is in alignment with your values and one that is on track with your higher purpose.

2. **You may need to go against the crowd to follow your intuition**. At times, it's tempting and sometimes easier to follow popular opinion when it comes to life choices, but what is your inner truth telling you? Is it different from what others are thinking, saying or doing? In today's world, it is no longer useful or wise to reference your opinion based on what others believe or think. History provides us with a multitude of examples where popular opinions have changed over time: the earth is flat – with new information – no, the earth is actually a sphere; smoking has health benefits – with new information – smoking is a health hazard.

    Today, the rapid spread of new information via social media and online communication is enabling increasingly swift changes in opinion. In recent times, public opinion has turned in relation to abuse of women, the historical abuse of children by clergy, and the plight of refugees. With the advent of Covid and the many narratives to negotiate, the importance of trusting one's personal knowing, has become essential. A tuned intuition can support an independent personal opinion. It is empowering to develop a deep sense of trust in yourself and navigate life based on what you feel to be true; to be sovereign in your beliefs and choices, rather than align automatically with prevailing ways of thinking.

3. **Your intuition is intimately linked to your creativity.** The same creative energy which moves through you, and all peoples of the Earth, has brought forward some of the greatest insight and new thought on the planet. Many wonderful inventions and significant problem-solving have emerged from this inner creative energy. It often comes in inspired moments or relaxed states in which the channels

are open for something *out of the box* to come through. Wouldn't you want access to this creative wisdom?

4. **Intuition is supported through embracing your emotions**. It is true that your emotions can act as part of your inner guidance system. By doing so, you are able to learn what your excitement, fear, anger or resistance is trying to communicate to you. Is it moving you toward or away from a choice? At times it can be the most subtle nuance of emotion that can indicate life direction for you.

    Though sometimes not considered an emotion, *love* can be a powerful guide for your choices and communicate the truth about any situation. It is the path of *going to the heart of the matter*. In addition, *compassion* for yourself and others is a vitally important heart-based emotion that will guide your life.

5. **Expanding your intuition is a lifetime process.** Connecting with your intuition is a process that will continually develop throughout your lifetime, if you pursue it. It certainly has been for me. There is a balance to be found between trusting yourself and following through with action. Small-safe-steps are often the best mode of action, which will build the platform within you for bigger leaps of faith as you progress. It is the step-by-step building of a deeper relationship with your innate knowing and Higher Self that connects you with the profound wisdom it offers and develops your trust in this guidance. This can sometimes be daunting yet will often lead you through a process of personal discovery, which is ultimately rewarding.

6. **Expect the unexpected.** I will say that as a young woman, I had no idea that my life would lead me towards the intuitive journey. In fact, I do not recall feeling particularly intuitive at all. However, life has a way of steering us along our higher path and this is what happened for me as my personal journey took a number of unexpected turns many years ago. It is the intuitive path I took, as I followed these shifts and

changes, which has made all the difference.

As you deepen the recognition and trust in your own intuition, you will build greater surety to follow its guidance. Sometimes the guidance may show up as the *unexpected* in your life, and you can experience the profound gifts it brings.

My Evolving Intuition

By the age of 21, I was managing the Medical Record Department of a major teaching hospital in Sydney and was responsible for 15 staff. I felt on track with my career. My heart was fully engaged in my contribution to the hospital as well as my role in delivering quality patient care and medical research services. Looking back, it was an enormous commitment for a young woman. It was a high-pressure, stressful position. On top of this, I was in the early stages of my marriage and we were already struggling, yet I was deeply in love.

A career colleague of mine, who I knew cared about my wellbeing, suggested I explore meditation as a form of stress management. She recommended I learn Transcendental Meditation (TM).[6] This idea kept playing on my mind and I began to feel it may be helpful. At this stage, I had no awareness of my intuition and zero personal development experience. I decided to go along to the TM Centre to learn this form of meditation, and from the moment the teacher whispered the special mantra in my ear, I was committed. I practiced 20 minutes, twice a day for the next five years. Meditation brought me inner peace and a rewarding retreat into myself. Ever since that time, I have meditated regularly, utilising a variety of practices over the years.

During the first year of meditating, I attended a TM retreat in the Blue Mountains, west of Sydney. The organisation owned a Meditation Centre there, nestled within a peaceful Australian bushland setting. The program included a daily dissertation by Maharishi Mahesh Yogi, the founder and creator of TM. Each day we sat together as a group and watched his video presentations in the meditation hall. Maharishi spoke about the *Seven Levels of Consciousness*[7] and I remember feeling I had no idea what he was talking about! At some point, while listening to his explanations, I experienced a realisation; there was so much more to awareness and life than I had been living. From this moment onward, I was passionately driven on a path of expanded consciousness in my life.

My husband and I steadily grew apart, and after five years of marriage, we separated. Devastated, I moved to a rural coastal area to be closer to my family and find my way forward. While reaching out for social connection, I was attracted to an advertisement in a local newspaper inviting new members to a study group for *A Course in Miracles (ACIM).*[8] I had never heard of the course nor its teachings. Over time, I discovered that ACIM was a channelled textbook based on the concept that *miracles are caused by a shift in our perception*, as well as *the healing power of inviting Spirit into our relationships.* I actively studied A Course in Miracles for the next two years, which involved daily meditations, plus weekly group gatherings to discuss experiences and understandings from the text. This was my first introduction to the concept that we are ultimately reflections of each other, and also understanding the healing force of welcoming a Higher Power (not based on any religious dictum) into my life.

During those two years, I also heard about a healing modality known as Rebirthing (now called Breathwork).[9] Rebirthing is a breathing technique that allows for deep insight into our personal life patterns and our spiritual connection. The word *Rebirthing* tweaked my interest - I was curious about the concept of exploring my emotions, understanding and releasing anything that might be in the way of experiencing life to the full.

Then, out of the blue, I was made redundant from my job. With time on my hands, I walked the local beach, praying for clarity on my best life choices going forward. I made the decision to sell my home, and the sale occurred incredibly quickly, contrary to a stagnant property market. I then made my way back to

Sydney. Within months of arriving, I participated in a weekend course called, *Loving Relationships Training*[10] and subsequently, a professional Rebirther training. During this program, and over the next several years, I journeyed deeply into emotional healing work, shame reduction, understanding relationship dynamics, and exploring bodywork and spiritual healing practices.

Throughout this phase of healing study, I experienced an expansion in my intuition. I found the more emotionally present I became, the more intuitive clarity I gained. I loved the aspect of me that simply knew things beyond what I could logically know. My intuition was also delivering a deep sense of being on track and on purpose, guiding me on a unique path I knew was right for me.

I was excited by the development of my intuition and, at the same time, its inner guidance told me that I could further hone and develop my skills. It was as if my intuition was actually guiding me to further expansion. By this stage, I was experienced in a variety of personal development processes and could see how to apply these to develop the relationship with my inner knowing. These practises are explained in this book.

After five years of delving deeply into emotional healing and personal development, I also began to experience a rapidly expanding psyche; this included an awareness of other dimensional realities. I found this quite disturbing and somewhat out of my control, so I began looking for ways to gain greater choice over what I was tuning into. This led me to reach out for assistance from a spiritual healer. The healer gave me a meditation and affirmation practise focused on my connection to a Higher Light and Higher Power.

Several days into this daily meditation practice, I experienced a spontaneous awakening to the loving presence of Angelic helpers - who are always with us (the full story is in Chapter 10 - Spiritual Assistance). As a result of this awakening, I became consciously aware of these helpers, and there was no doubt in my mind who they were. It was a wholly loving experience. From that moment onward, I embraced the presence of my Angelic support team who assist, guide and support my life daily. They have brought a whole new dimension to the development of, and confidence in, my intuition.

This breakthrough in my psyche was also a catalyst for me to understand our subtle energy system, chakras, multi-dimensional reality and ultimately to gain mastery over my expanded awareness. I discovered that our energy system contains the patterns of our life, based on our past experience, and these patterns influence our behaviours, current life interactions, and the clarity of our intuition. This also culminated in my ability to intuit the life patterning that people hold in their energy system and which affect their relationships, health, work, purpose or other aspects of their life.

As a result of my refined intuition, I also developed the capacity to intuit the underlying patterning of disease in the body – a form of Medical Intuition. This arose as a natural progression of deepening my intuition and became complimentary to my knowledge of physiology and nutritional biology. It is often the case that our learned skills will complement our intuition.

As I reflect back over my life, I see how my intuition was guiding me even through those early years. I just didn't recognise or see it that way at the time. From the recurring inner nudges to study meditation, to my attraction to the Course in Miracles work. Then my interest in rebirthing and my ongoing thirst for personal development, followed by my drive to understand the human energy system. My intuition guided me every step of the way for purposeful life expansion. And it can do so for you too.

For over 30 years I have passionately pursued a deep and rewarding relationship with my intuition. When inspired to write *An Intuitive Life*, I knew I must explain the foundational elements of deep intuition first. For some people, these elements may appear very basic, but they build the all-important foundation for further learning. For example, I remember my dance teachers would insist I have the basic steps of dance well integrated before I could glide around the dance floor with grace, ease and beauty. At times, I would feel bored with those basics yet continued with them as a path to mastery. The intuitive basics are your foundational steps to achieving intuitive mastery.

Therefore, I encourage you to understand the value of the fundamentals outlined in the early chapters of this book. They are the base stones for experiencing a deep and rewarding relationship with your intuition. At the same time, feel free to jump ahead if you are drawn to do so, as developing intuition is not a linear experience.

*The first and most effective step
for connecting with your intuition
is to use your intention.*

2.
Foundations for Intuitive Mastery

Your Intuition is your inner guidance system. This innate knowing emerges from a creative place within your consciousness. It is not from rational or logical thought, though its messages can be contemplated and sometimes understood in this way. Instead, it rides on your emotions or feelings and has a broad range of *voices* that speak in a variety of ways. These can be different for each individual. Some people experience *a sense* or *gut feeling*, others receive a *sign* or *vision*, while many simply have a *knowing*. Through understanding and recognising the many voices of intuition, you can become familiar with your own unique repertoire.

In addition, intuitive messages have a certain *ring* or *feeling* tone, which you can learn to identify as your special voice from within. You can develop a relationship with the unique *tonality* of your inner wisdom. This is a major key to discerning intuitive messages in your life, as opposed to just another piece of information within your world. However, whether you are aware of it or not, you are already in touch with your intuition to some degree and using it in your daily life choices.

These include: what to have for dinner, the colour of a new piece of clothing, the perfect birthday gift to buy a friend, choosing a new hairdresser, coordinating a social gathering, which movie to see, which music to listen to, where you would like to holiday, social activities you want to attend, as well as a myriad of daily business and work choices. Regarding your work, it could be intuiting the best timing to follow up with clients, prioritising workload, marketing choices, staff selection, raising something you *see* needs to be handled, reminding people if you have *a feeling* that they may have missed something, checking back on details of work projects because you have *a sense* you should follow up on them.

It is important to embrace awareness of your intuition in the simplest aspects of your daily life because this establishes the foundation for greater creative flow. By enjoying the minutia of its ever-present guidance, you can not only have fun with it, but also build your receptiveness to those pivotal moments which play out a grand design in your life.

Remember, intuition is a vibrational alignment with what you truly want, and you make choices based on what you want every day. So, your feelings are a centrepiece because intuition rides on your feelings and emotions, and these motivate you *toward* or *away from* certain life choices. The many aspects of emotional guidance are discussed in the next chapter.

Benefits of following your intuition

Your intuition is designed to lead you on the path of least resistance. Following your intuition can make life easier and invoke the feeling of being in the *flow* or *reaching a sweet spot*. This state is experienced as a sense of happy satisfaction about how things are unfolding in your life.

Trusting and following your intuition will lead to a happier life, allow magic to happen, and keep you on purpose with your highest good. Your intuition knows the bigger picture beyond what is obvious or in front of you, and if you learn to listen and follow it, good things, even astounding things, will happen.

Even more rewarding is to develop your intuition, so it encompasses all aspects of your life and becomes a natural part of your daily experience. Being in this daily flow of intuitive guidance can bring deep satisfaction and life fulfilment. It's the simple yet profound things, such as *who you were guided to be in touch with today* or *what choices you felt compelled to make*, which can lead you on the path of benevolent receiving and contribution in your life.

Reflecting on others' real-life stories of intuition, from the most mundane to the more complex, will help you establish greater intuitive recognition in your own life. Here are a few stories from women responding to their everyday inner guidance.

Everyday intuition stories

Jenny - A beneficial Career Change

"I was offered a prestigious, highly paid job without applying for it and *instantly knew* it was the right thing for me to accept – it took a week for my logical mind to catch up. Accepting the position meant a complete move between cities, which was something I had not contemplated or planned. I made the move four weeks later, and I haven't looked back. It was one of the best intuitive decisions I ever made."

Rose - Rewards at Work

"As a primary school teacher, I use my intuition to guide my teaching style on a daily basis. I seem to know when a child has understood a concept or when they are struggling. I choose to stay aware of my intuition when probing and watching where they are up to and often change my approach or explanation or even rearrange my lesson on the spot to follow these feelings. It is such a joy to see a child grasp a new idea or skill, and this reinforces my belief in following my gut feelings."

Robyn -Travel Plans Sorted

"I felt strongly I wanted to attend an important business meeting in another city, but I also wanted to visit and stay with a close friend who lived about 35 kms away from the meeting venue. There were no trains to the venue location and a taxi would have been very expensive. I decided to trust my impetus to go and that travel details would work out. I booked a flight and arranged the accommodation with my friend. When I arrived at her home, I discovered there was a bus route that ran from 20 metres outside her front door and then, via a windy route, ended 50 metres from the meeting venue!"

The downside of not following your intuition

Equally, there is a downside to ignoring your inner guidance. Perhaps you feel resistant to following your intuition as its guidance makes no rational sense. Or you may question it, fear its messages, and take no action. At times, you might simply dismiss it and turn your back on the subtle messages you've received, even the recurring ones.

However, if you ignore your intuition, it can lead to unnecessary struggle and resistance in your life; it always pays to listen! The following are some first-hand stories of what happened when these women did not listen to their intuition.

Deanna - A Missed Opportunity

"Once I saw a unit for sale in the same block as mine, and I resisted the idea of buying it based on the cost. My intuition kept knocking at the door in a variety of ways, but I was too scared to listen. I had recently purchased my first property six months earlier and was not confident or comfortable to make another buy so soon. All it would have taken was some research and number crunching, then it would have been a no-brainer to buy at the time. I let my fear get in the way of my intuition, so much so that I didn't take the time to consider gathering all the facts. If only I had, it's worth three times as much now."

Julie - Lost Earrings

"As a fashion stylist, I enjoy the personal expression of unique clothes and accessories. When I wear earrings that have no secure backs, I have sometimes thought as I put them on to make them more secure, but do not listen to that message - and then I lose them. These are times when my inner voice speaks quietly about small details, but I don't quite take it seriously. This has happened on three occasions over several years, and I have subsequently lost some much-loved earrings. Each time I am very annoyed with myself for not listening to that little voice."

Sue - It's Just Not Rational

"I had purchased some silver coin as an investment, and for a range of reasons had not picked them up from the company. Many months went by, and I had received several *messages* in my life to either go and collect the coins or sell them. It didn't seem rational to sell as the price had declined, but even so, I kept feeling to take action and yet ignored it. It turned out I missed an e-mail from the company saying they would charge me for storage if I did not collect the silver. I received an account for $105 for the storage, which they would not waive. It would definitely have paid to follow up those subtle messages I had been receiving."

Premise for our intuition

The underlying premise I use regarding intuition is that you are connected to a greater source of Divine Energy or Higher Self that is loving, benevolent, and all-knowing. This source can be called God, Higher Self, Energy, One Heart, Yahweh, Universe, Light, Divine Source or other spiritual names. You are *one* with this ever-creative energy which moves through you via your desires. Living in alignment with that creative flow involves being alert to your desires. You can ask yourself, *"What do I desire?"* whenever you tune in to your intuition. This offers a request to your intuition to guide you - via what you want on a material level, and also on a soul level. Intuition, therefore, is creative energy moving through you, and you can learn to live more in alignment with that creative flow by being *intentional*.

The first step is intention

The first and most effective step for connecting with your intuition is to use your *intention* to create alignment. Intention is one of the most powerful personal development tools you can utilise. Simply choosing to read about the intuitive process, in books such as the one you're reading, is a form of intention that will deepen your intuition. However, it is even more potent to be directional about it and state your intent aloud.

Stating your intention focuses your conscious desire towards a particular outcome. For example, *"I intend to be more in tune with my intuition."* Intention has a spiritual aspect that focuses the energy of your Higher Self directly into the area of life in which you need assistance. It is like a laser beam of light shining through and energising that part of your existence.

You can use intention to initiate improvement or experience a positive shift in any aspect of your life. Once you identify what you want, you can state an intention. In this instance, the focus of your intent is on developing your intuitive capacities.

Your intention is best spoken aloud

This assists your mind to focus on what you want and brings your intent into physical form, using the vibration of your spoken word. If you accept the concept that your words have power, then speaking your intent aloud increases the potency of that energy.

Your intention statements to focus your intuition could be like any of the following:

"I intend to connect more deeply with my intuition."

"I intend to hear my intuition more clearly."

"I intend to strengthen my intuitive knowing."

"I intend to connect with my higher knowing."

"I intend a clear and open connection with my innate knowing."

You could add the following intention to hear your intuition more clearly:

"Speak to me in ways I can understand. I intend the presence of being to recognise the messages and the courage to take action."

Intention need not be complicated. It really is that easy – use your own words with heartfelt desire according to what you would like to achieve. Do this and you will start or increase the flow. This process is simply you talking to your own being and consciousness at this point.

Setting intention

Find a quiet place where you can speak your intention to connect with your intuition aloud. It's best to choose a place where you can be calm and focused. You can do this by sitting in meditation, going into nature, or perhaps sitting quietly on a veranda in the sun. Breathe deeply, fully and gently. When settled, ask aloud for your Higher Knowing to move through you.

You can start by using one of the intentions listed above or create your own.

Do this exercise as often as you feel moved to do so.

Note: It is not necessary to be this ceremonial about your intention, however initially it can help to set the scene for some quiet, focused time to speak your conscious intent to connect. You could also speak your intention at any time during the course of your day, such as during a morning walk, in the shower, during lunch time, or anytime when you can focus your mind on your intent and say it aloud.

At any point in your life journey, you can restate your intention for deepening your innate knowing

The development of your intuition will be an ever-evolving life process with expanding dimensions of connection and increasing rewards over time. There may be points along your journey where you know and feel you can go deeper. The utilisation of intent can be primary to the next level of expansion. Simply go back to this most basic process of speaking aloud your intent to connect and go deeper.

Being specific

You can also use intention to be *in tune* with your intuition on *specific* subjects. For example, if you have choices to make in your life and you are looking for direction, you can ask for signs and ask to be led to the choice that is for your highest good.

For example:

"I intend to know right action regarding .... *life choice / issue*.... Please make the signs clear for me."

"I intend the choice for my highest good regarding .... *life choice / issue*...."

Use your own words, believe and breathe

Using your own words is the most beneficial way to express your intention. You can start with the suggestions above and allow your own statements to evolve. There is a feedback cycle that can happen between your intuition and your words. As you learn to tune in and listen, you will be guided to the most beneficial words to use for your own psyche – they sit right when you say them. Remember though, it is ultimately your intent that gives your words their potency.

It is also important that you *mean it* when you speak your intent. This is sometimes known as *pure intent*; meaning to speak your intent wholeheartedly and from your centre. Choose to *believe* you will receive a result - your belief is key. When you state an intention, it is helpful to breathe in after you state it aloud and imagine receiving the connection to your intuitive knowing. Your breath is your link to Creative Source that is constantly moving through you. In this way, your breath is a connection pathway to your Higher Knowing. In fact, your breath is symbolic of receiving in general.

Intuition and Logic

Another foundation for expanded intuition is understanding the interplay between your logical mind and your intuitive self. Many people believe that intuition has very little relationship to logic, but nothing could be further from the truth. Intuition married harmoniously with logic can be a powerful creative duo in your life.

It is true that over-zealous logic can get in the way of trusting and following your intuitive knowing. In fact, your innate knowing is completely separate from your logical mind. Intuition emanates from a broader awareness that lies within your entire being. Over time, though, you can develop co-operation, or a *confluence*, of your logical mind, your heart and your intuition to form a powerful combined guidance system.[11]

Rely a little on logic

As you build your intuitive confidence, it pays to rely on your logic to some degree. You can also use past experience to interpret whether your perceived intuition is on track.

For example, you might wake up one morning and feel like taking the day off:

Scenario 1: At the same time, you are aware that completing your list of important 'to-do's' will give you a sense of peace at the end of the day. You may choose to go with the logic of getting the job done, knowing that this will leave you more peaceful. Intuition is guiding you toward peace of mind.

Scenario 2: Perhaps you know you have been overworking, feeling a little stressed and on edge – so you choose to take the day off despite the to-do list. In this case, your logic would understand that you need to take care of yourself and keep your life in balance. Your intuition is guiding you toward this outcome.

Balance is the key to marrying logic and intuition. Your logic can also play a helpful role in taking small-safe-steps in your intuitive development.

Education complements intuition

Your experience, education and a little research can be very handy in working with your intuition.

Vicki - Investment Win

"Within a few months of moving to a new city, I purchased my first property, based on my intuition and backed by having studied the real estate market for the previous five years. I wasn't considering purchasing at the time, but the unit I was renting came on the market and another buyer expressed interest. I made an instant intuitive decision, "I am going to buy it" ... and I did. I happened to love the unit, especially as I was its first tenant. Subsequently, I was madly researching information to confirm my intuition and ensure I was buying in the right place for the best price. On five separate occasions, I received *messages* via other people over a six-week period, which continued to reassure me I had made a good decision. It has proven to be the perfect place to find myself - surrounded by the things I love - cafes, art galleries, and homeware design shops, and is close to the day-to-day amenities I need...food, transport, restaurants. Everything is in walking distance – the city, my hairdresser, the movies - I love it!"

The following are two great examples of intuition married with logic. For both these women, they experienced an original, inspired idea followed by logical steps, including a plan to enhance personal skills. In addition, they followed through on opportunities that came their way, which opened the door to greater outcomes in both situations.

Nicole - Passion for Fashion

"I was working for a successful events company as a corporate executive. My job was secure, and I felt rewarded, having completed many successful event projects. However, I had a passion for fashion since my teenage years, and a lifetime desire to work in the industry. Because of this, I had been developing my skills through part-time study in fashion. I was experiencing a rising impetus to be working and expressing my creativity in this manner. My desire became so strong I decided to take a leap of faith and move into part-time work, which involved less secure income but provided time to focus on the possibilities of a fashion career.

The very first week of my new routine, I was offered a volunteer role on a local Fashion Week project, and through that connection decided to put my name down for future volunteer programs. I received a phone call out of the blue to work on another advertising project in fashion, and through that job I met the business owner. He subsequently offered me opportunities to work within the fashion industry as a stylist assistant, as well as managing the volunteer program for key fashion events. Later, I was given free tickets to a 5-day fashion show where I was asked to write a daily blog about the events. I was so joyous and excited about the unfolding of my life in fashion, feeling right in the sweet spot of my vision and experiencing a dream come true.

I continued to explore my love of fashion through establishing my own business. My services included personal styling consultations, seeing clients for wardrobe makeovers, and assisting people to establish an authentic expression of themselves through design. Although I loved this work, eventually the challenges of running a business led me to decide on a return to my other area of expertise, events management. Even though my original fashion dream was not fully realised, I had been able to experience the merging of two creative talents – fashion and events.

My life feels forever enriched by taking those brave steps and living out some of my fashion goals."

Melissa - Plans for a Career Move

"My intuition has recently been fuelling a sense of excitement about my future. I've been asking myself how I can increase my income and better plan for my retirement. It has felt like an unobtainable goal. Daily life can be stressful as a single parent with full-time work, school fees, expenses for my teenage son and weekly living costs that seem to be ever increasing. Progress didn't seem possible, but I had this constant feeling there must be a way to make my dreams happen. I knew it was important to plan for when my son left home. Things would need to change to make these plans come true.

I decided to apply for a promotion, which meant I would need to leave my hometown and take a job in the country. This seemed like something that would keep me busy (so I didn't miss my son!) and give me an opportunity to reach my financial goals. The job would mean significantly increased income as well as free accommodation, which would greatly reduce my living expenses.

I worked hard for nearly eight months preparing and putting everything in place to make this my reality. I was accepted into a training program and made some excellent contacts. Through those contacts, I was offered a great job within a few hours driving distance of my friends and family, so I took the leap of faith. Now, I can focus on reaching my financial goals."

This is a perfect example of intuition guiding life direction (desire for better retirement plan) and then doing the due diligence and taking action (applying for promotion and doing further training) for the flow and synchronicities to happen (acceptance into the training and making helpful contacts).

Blending professional skills and artistic flair

Education and intuition can also combine in the application of certain skills or professions that involve craftsmanship; of course, craftsmanship emerges from the creative source of intuition.

A carpenter will use their skill and expertise in building a house and combine this with an innate sense around design, timing and choice of materials. A graphic designer will use their talents on the computer, and technical understanding of colour combinations and layout, and apply these skills alongside their intuitive artistic design on the project. A good health practitioner will merge their education and experience, together with their intuition, to deliver the best care options for a patient at any given time.

Christina - Intuitive Health Care

"As a natural health practitioner, my intuition assists me when I suspect a patient may have a more serious health problem than is immediately obvious. I will experience a gut feeling to refer that person for further medical investigation and have found myself accurate on several occasions. One patient presented with recurring back pain who, on referral, was diagnosed with stomach cancer, which was then effectively treated. Another patient was experiencing ongoing painful ear issues and general malaise despite a visit to her doctor and being treated with ear drops. One night, I awoke at 2 am with the thought that she had Auricular (inner ear) Shingles. My patient went back to her doctor, the diagnosis was confirmed, and she subsequently recovered."

The importance of little things

Even in the basic activities of life, such as baking a cake or cooking a meal, we can use the combination of the recipe (logic) with our creative intuitive flair (adding a pinch of this and a pinch of that).

Where are you currently combining your creativity with your knowledge in your life? If you tune into and acknowledge the intuitive aspect you already use in your daily life, you will expand your intuition and learn to further trust your ability.

Intuition with no logic at all

Sometimes your intuition will have no logic at all, and yet you will know to follow it.

For example, you might have the last $20 in your wallet and yet feel compelled to spend it on buying a meal for someone in need. Perhaps you decide you need to take a week off to visit your family or a good friend, even though you have a busy schedule. However, you simply feel strongly that you need to spend time with them.

You may only see in retrospect the benevolent guidance within your intuition.

Andrea - Told To Go Home

"I was given the afternoon off work, which provided me several hours of free time. I was excited about the concept of extra time, as I had plenty of things to do, including some much-needed shopping or possibly catching up with a friend. As I started driving away from work, I noticed I felt strongly I simply wanted to go home and hide. This was illogical and I thought to myself, "That's strange" and questioned myself a little, however, the feeling persisted. I decided to trust my desire and drove directly home. Fifteen minutes after arriving home and parking my car in the garage, a huge storm including hail arrived. I was very happy to be safely tucked away inside my house with my car secure from risk of damage."

Letting go of logic

As mentioned, logic is not your intuition. It is a helpful reference point - sometimes. Indeed, logic can get in the way of trusting your intuition. This usually happens when there is a battle between what we *feel* about a choice and what we *think* about it. Your mind might be telling you one thing and your feelings or heart another.

Some basic life examples:

You feel strongly you would like to participate in an educational program, or perhaps attend some live entertainment, but your logic is telling you that it's out of your budget.

You feel the urge to go to the beach for the morning, but your logic says the house needs cleaning.

Your gut feeling is warning you that a situation is not as it appears on the surface. This may require letting go of what is presented and trusting your feeling instead.

Only you are going to be able to discern the best choices on each occasion and your choice may end up being outside the logic of the situation. This is where intuitive discernment comes into play.

Practical Steps for Intuitive Discernment

1. State your intention to connect with your intuition.

Please follow the steps outlined in this chapter. This is one of the most important foundational actions you can take for deepening your intuition.

2. When you feel stuck between choices, a helpful exercise is to *sit with* each option for a while and experience how each choice *feels* to you:

Ask yourself:

How does it feel to say yes? Does it give me energy? Does it feel a happy choice? Do I feel expanded or contracted around that choice? Is this choice based in self-love?

How does it feel to say no? Does it give me energy? Does it feel a happy choice? Do I feel expanded or contracted around that choice? Is this choice based in self-love?

You could sit with the 'yes' and the 'no' for an hour, a day or even a week each, to help gain clarity on how you feel.

When you have completed this process, you may like to explore choosing what gives you the most energy and happiness, but remember, you can't get it wrong.

In the following example, this woman has developed the skill to check in with her feelings, the response in her body, and the alignment with her core values.

Margaret - Does It Feel Right?

"Over many years, I have learned to integrate my intuition into my everyday way of being, which now means I don't even think about my intuition. Even within the basics of when to go shopping, phone people, exercise, what to eat, or which route to take when driving my grandchildren to school. These choices inevitably result in flow and ease.

With big decisions, I usually pause and not rush into anything. *If it feels good and right*, and I don't feel any resistance to the action or choice, then I know it's on track for me.

Sometimes the outcome is not what I wanted, and I ask myself - what is it within me that I need to learn from this? Alternatively, I will experience a recognition that it was a better outcome for me overall.

This has been a process of training myself over thirty years of not *just going with what I think, but rather with what I feel about what I think, and also what is the response in my body as I feel and think these things.* Are these thoughts, feelings and response in my body in alignment, or is there discord? Is this choice in alignment with my spiritual values - empathy, generosity, and compassion? It's important to me that compassion and generosity are the foundations of my life on an everyday basis."

Margaret's story depicts an integration of checking with herself, trusting in the flow of things, and embracing the value of personal integrity in the intuitive process. It also demonstrates that following your intuition is not always about having the outcome you want, but rather trusting in the process and what unfolds.

3. To gain clarity on the best choice, you can ask yourself - What is in my heart? And consciously tune in to the truth within your heart centre. In this way, you are asking your heart to *speak* to you and building an aware connection with your heart's knowingness.

You may need to allow some time for your heart's truth to rise to your awareness. This could be anywhere from immediate clarity, to days, a week, or longer. Any delay may be related to the best timing for you to know, or sometimes it simply takes time to come to terms with how we truly feel. Please refer to Chapter 4 – Going to the Heart of the Matter – for a deeper understanding of the guidance from your heart.

If you are contemplating a particularly important life choice, you could use some of the intuition tools in the following chapters to gain clarity on what you want.

4. There are many other tips for intuitive discernment outlined throughout this book. I'll cover these as additional items in the related chapters.

*Your feelings can be rich
with intuitive communication
and a pathway to your Greater Knowing.*

3.

Your Emotions Are the Key

As mentioned, your feelings and emotions are the direct connection to your intuition. This sounds simple enough, but many people struggle to recognise emotions or understand what they are feeling. Yet, the more you can embrace your feelings, the more in tune you will be with your inner guidance system. Your feelings are the freeway or vibrational pathway to your Higher Self and Higher Knowing; that part of you which knows everything and to which you are connected beyond time and space. Your Higher Self knows the potential of what's ahead for you. Even though you can't see it, you may *feel* it.

Of course, your feelings are not always intuitive communication. Sometimes your emotions will be an authentic response to a life situation, such as loss, shock, change of circumstances, success or love. Emotions can be incredibly complex with multiple layers of experience. Some experts make a distinction between feelings being an *internal experience* and emotions being the *outward expression*. So, you may have a nuance of an inner feeling such as a hunch, sense of resistance or twinge of excitement, or you may experience a full-blown emotional expression such as fear, sorrow, anger, joy, raucous laughter or driving passion.

At times, our emotions may be what we feel more comfortable with rather than our true feelings. Our true feelings are the reality of what we feel *deep* inside, however these may lie behind what we initially allow our self to acknowledge. We may be out of tune with our true feelings because of past experiences, family influences or societal pressures that have not provided a safe place for their expression. As a result, some people become more comfortable with certain feelings as opposed to others. For example, they may be safe expressing their anger more than their fear or sadness, or others may be more comfortable with their sadness as opposed to their anger. I further explain the concept of how our experiences affect what we feel and the clarity of our intuition in Chapter 8, 'Intuition versus Fantasy'.

The more you embrace your feelings and emotions and give them a voice, the more you will come into balance with them. This will assist you to receive the guidance they may offer. With balance, your feelings can be rich with intuitive communication and provide a pathway to your Greater Knowing. Please refer to the practical steps at the end of this chapter for ways to embrace and work with your emotions.

Anger or feelings of resistance

You may find that feelings of anger or resistance are actually your intuition telling you to say *"No"* to something or someone. By saying *"No"*, you thereby set a healthy personal boundary or make a change for the better in life. Resistance could be intuition saying, *"Hang on a minute, I'm not sure this is the best choice for me."* For example, you may not feel like attending a particular function or event and choose to say, *"No,"* even though you would usually go, and people expect you to be there. However, not attending could simply be a better choice for you at this time. Feeling angry about the behaviour of your children could be telling you to set healthier limits with them. Feeling annoyed at someone's repetitive actions could be telling you it is time to speak up and express how you feel. Or perhaps you feel resistant towards purchasing an item someone is trying to sell you – inwardly you know it is not the right choice for you. There are many possible situations where experiencing resistance could be your gut feelings saying, *"No."*

Remember, resistance, even in its finest nuance, can be guidance. Learn to trust this aspect of yourself, because developing a relationship with this part of your emotional body can save you a great deal of time and angst.

Jenny - Shopping Made Easy

"I can't tell you how many times I have felt resistant to driving to the shops even though I had my shopping list ready, but decided to trust the *"No."* Invariably, the next day something important is added to the list, and this saves me valuable time by avoiding a double journey to the supermarket."

Tracey - Business Decision was Being Guided to Say "No"

"I had a strong feeling to not trust a consultant who approached me to do some work via my organisation. She had already secured funding for the work but needed an incorporated association to receive the money. I noticed I kept feeling resistant to her request, however, a couple of my staff thought the project was quite good. Against my inner knowing, I proceeded with the arrangement. Eight weeks later, she disappeared with $30,000 of misappropriated funds. My organisation had to cover this amount."

Rachel - Time to Change Behaviour

"I was on holidays and noticed I was spending all my time getting things done on my 'to-do' list. I started to feel angry that there was no time to simply rest and be. One day, when talking about this with a friend, I realised how angry and frustrated I felt about my lack of free time and felt this was a strong message to change my behaviour, come into balance and factor in some holiday down-time for myself."

Patricia - Something Was Not Quite Right

"Looking back on my life, I realise I have experienced good intuitive discernment from quite a young age. When I was around 12 years old, my mother became newly involved with a local church group in our small coastal town. The church had an associated youth group, and the youth group leader was very proactive in getting to know young people in town. He started to drop by our home unannounced and uninvited, sometimes when my mother was not home. He would linger on his visits and make himself comfortable on the lounge. I found him abhorrent and hypocritical and felt invaded by his unannounced visits during which he expected my attention. I wasn't very polite to him, and my mother told me she didn't want me to be rude. But I couldn't help it, every part of me said, "No," and I didn't have any other capacities except to be rude. Eventually, he stopped dropping by.

Ten to fifteen years later, my mother received a phone call from the police. This particular youth worker was being investigated for paedophile activity and the police were enquiring if she was aware of any past untoward behaviour by him."

Penny - Intuitive Radar

"I have now been a complementary health practitioner for the past 22 years and find I use my intuitive radar on a daily basis. I have built faith in my intuitive discernment over the years through layers of experience of either *trusting* or *not trusting* my knowing.

It is particularly sharp if I have a feeling that a patient has a potential reason, either consciously or subconsciously, to resist their recovery. On occasion, someone may be more invested in their story of ill health than in getting better. This situation rarely arises, but when it does present itself, I can pick it a mile away. It is a distinct feeling of me being uncomfortable, or something feeling not quite right, with their story. My experience is there is a sense of resistance in the space, and that these people do not respond well to treatment."

Wendy - The "No" Can Sometimes Come With Strong Feelings

"It was New Year's Eve, and I received a call from friends, who were visiting from overseas for a few days, so we arranged to meet in the city to celebrate. I had a very clear intuitive *gut feeling* that said, *"No, don't go,"* and it came with a sense of feeling quite sick in my stomach. I wanted to meet up with my friends, but I also wanted to trust myself. I struggled for several hours with this combat in my mind and emotions and convinced myself to go out because 'it was New Year's Eve after all.'

I had a drink while I was getting ready, caught a train to town, and went looking for my friends at our agreed meeting place. Naturally, there were huge numbers of people out celebrating, and I wondered how I would ever find them - and I didn't. I gave up the search and decided to go home. I walked downtown and had a drink, just one. I met up with a small group of three to four people, and we decided to have a ride on one of the entertainment rides. I said goodbye to them and walked to the railway station to go home. I never made it home that night. I don't remember much of what happened after that. I woke up in hospital on New Year's Day. The nurses said I had been really drunk and perhaps drugged. I had no money as my bag had been stolen. Luckily, it had only contained keys and twenty dollars. Fortunately, my sister was available to collect me."

Author's note: Resisting your intuition does not necessarily have such dramatic outcomes, but this is a good example of how inner knowing can be very aware of what might be ahead.

Facing your fears

Always honour fear – it is telling you something.

Sometimes following your intuition can trigger feelings of fear. Perhaps fear of rejection or fear of making the wrong decision. Fear of following your inner guidance can simply be due to a lack of familiarity with and trust in that voice within you. While you are in the process of building familiarity with your intuition, you may struggle with distinguishing between when to trust your fear as a warning signal, compared to moments when fear is holding you back from something exciting.

Turning inward and exploring the feelings of fear around your choices will enable you to notice nuanced differences in these messages. For example, fear can be interpreted as a warning to remove yourself from a situation or to be careful, as in the New Year's Eve story above. On the other hand, it could be telling you that there is the possibility of something good or exciting ahead. Perhaps a situation only seems scary because it is outside your comfort zone? You can learn to gain safety and familiarity with your intuition by taking small-safe-steps and learning finer distinctions around feelings of fear through trial and error.

Ava - When Fear Turns to Excitement

"A friend had organised an abseiling outing in our local National Park. I had never been abseiling nor desired to go previously but felt excited at the prospect of a new adventure. Our first drop was down a straight-faced natural rock wall. Although my heart was racing as I made this first drop, it felt relatively safe and easy to achieve. The second drop, however, was across an overhang where I had to push out into mid-air to get beyond the lip of the rock and onto the rock face beneath. The thought of flying free out in the air over that lip upped the ante of my fear. Of course, after some trepidation, I launched into the air, and down the wall I went. I was filled with exhilaration and personal satisfaction that came from pushing past my fear and achieving something completely different and out of my comfort zone."

In this story, the initial guidance of excitement to go abseiling was then challenged by some fear during the event as she pushed through her comfort levels.

Maeve - When Fear Leads to Destiny

"At the beginning of the year, I felt a deep desire to travel somewhere special. I found myself thinking about one of my dream trips - to walk the Camino track in Spain (an ancient pilgrimage trail). Only weeks later, a friend asked me if I would like to go to Europe with her in May. I immediately felt excited and said, *"Yes,"* but then spent two to three months not taking any action towards the trip. Weeks and months went by, and yet my thoughts were caught up in daily work activities and reasons why I couldn't go. Making the arrangements and finding the money seemed very overwhelming. I had no obvious funds to travel, yet at the same time, I was receiving positive feedback and encouragement from my parents and friends about the idea. I also had that strong yearning for this special trip.

I could see that my fear and resistance were getting in the way of my excitement, so decided to push forward with my plans and focus on how I could actually do the trip. Situations and events started to unfold to make the trip possible. A colleague suddenly resigned, which delivered me the opportunity to earn a significant amount of additional income from covering her work. I finally completed my previous year's taxes and received a tax refund. I then won $2,500 in an online competition. My parents offered to 'make a donation' towards it, and I had work and money coming in from a variety of amazing sources. I couldn't ignore these signs.

In addition, I kept noticing messages on websites that appeared to say, "Walk the Camino." It was almost bizarre. A final sign that convinced me I was on the right path was my singing teacher suggesting a song I had never heard before called, "Defying Gravity,"[12] The words go something like this:

> "Too late for second guessing,
> too late to go back to sleep.
> It's time to trust my instincts,
> close my eyes...and leap!"

Hence, I was off to Europe, the Camino walk and a trip of a lifetime."

Practical ways to deal with fear

Practicing small-safe-steps, such as taking action within less impactful areas of your life, and using logic to work with your intuition, can build your faith in its power. In the example above, Ava followed her excitement to go abseiling within the context of a relatively safe situation. This experience led to a reference point where she learned that *on the other side of fear* was the possibility of a sense of exhilaration.

Another method of responding to fear is by *watching out for synchronicities* in life to lead the way. Aspects of life seemingly *falling into place* can be validation and guidance to take action.

Maeve's Camino walk story shows how circumstances flowed together in several magical ways to support this woman's desire for a special travel experience.

Taking small-safe-steps towards following your intuition is covered in more depth in the next chapter. Later chapters also discuss further how to work with synchronicities to complement your intuition. By using these processes, you can build familiarity with your intuitive voice and your sense of safety in following its guidance.

Passion and excitement leave clues

Your intuition may move through you in the form of passion, excitement, attraction to a particular event or item, desire or feeling motivated to action. These emotions can guide you towards the best action or direction to take – one that is the most fulfilling or most efficient for you.

Inspired ideas which cross your mind can also be your intuition speaking. Even if the inspiration is as basic as buying an extra cucumber at the market or an unplanned grocery item, learn to trust the simple things. You will find that it can be very convenient down the track to have trusted your intuition even in making simple decisions.

Your passion may speak in a variety of ways. You may feel excited to learn a new skill, moved to go out in nature for the day or inspired to see a particular movie. Perhaps, you experience a desire to spend time with a particular friend or to phone someone to see how they are going. You may feel drawn to participate in a specific training program or toward a holiday at a certain destination. These are all instances where your passions, inspirations and desires can be your inner knowing guiding you to fulfilling choices.

Janice - An Inspired Mother's Solution

"My 15-year-old son had been overseas for six months on a school exchange program and he started exploring all the things teenagers do – parties, dating, having some alcohol, being exposed to drugs. As the time for his return approached, my intuition told me that I needed to find a way for him to be able to explore life in a safe manner, while not straying too far from home. I discussed this desire with a friend, and she suggested I convert a room at home into a 'man cave.' This idea immediately struck me as the right solution. I was able to acquire some great furniture at low cost via e-bay, including a three-in-one games table for the centre of the room, eight red stools, and a flat screen television. We painted the walls, laid carpet tiles, added a couch, bean bags, bar fridge, dart board, lighting and a music system.

I presented the 'cave' to him for his fifteenth birthday, and he absolutely loved it! It was a private place to retreat with his friends who came over to hang out, play table games and watch TV; all in the safety of my home and not too far away from supervision. He also had several small 'cave' parties.

This inspired idea provided an incredible arm of support to this phase of my son's adolescence and increased peace of mind for me."

Excitement can point to greater things for us

As children, our natural passion, excitement and joyful expectation bubble forth easily. But, as we walk through life, experience challenges and disappointments, it's easy to lower our sights and reduce, or even lose, our dreams for a greater future. However, following our excitement can lead us to wonderful gifts in life. That's why it's important to notice when the feeling of excitement moves within and take time to embrace and explore all it offers.

Gina - Time Out with Bobby

"I had been retrenched from my job of 13 years, which, though not a total surprise, was very destabilising and upsetting to me and my family. I had received a reasonable payout but had children and a partner to support, so I needed to be strategic about my plans going forward. My partner and I had purchased a 20-acre property five years earlier, and I noticed all I really wanted to do was take care of the kids and work on our property for three months. I decided to trust this feeling moving through me.

I am a woman who enjoys working with tools and machines and being outside in the yard and garden. I kept feeling strongly that I wanted to purchase a Bobcat excavator so that I could tidy up the property and start some preparations for our new house site. The cost was around $16,000 and that would cut in deeply to the payout I had received, which made me feel a little nervous. Despite this concern, I found myself looking at advertisements for Bobcats and eventually I took the plunge and bought one. I absolutely loved getting out on the property and working with 'Bobby' (the Bobcat). I was able to do ten times as much in an hour than I could achieve with hand tools, and I realised that I could sell it down the track and essentially have done all the property development at little or no cost. Later that year, I went back to full-time work and a demanding schedule and was so pleased I had trusted my inner guidance to take time out, nurture my family and myself, and work the land."

When you are driven by your passion, the Universe can move mountains to back you in your choice to follow it.

Zara - A Peak Experience

"During my twenties, I had an absolute passion for outdoor adventure – I spent all my spare time hiking to remote areas, mountain biking, rock climbing, adventure racing and mountaineering, with equally dedicated and adventurous friends. I loved being enveloped within massive landscapes, often involving severe exposure to the elements.

One of the men in my climbing group shared his vision of an ambitious expedition to summit Denali (Mt. McKinley) in Alaska. Denali, located near the Arctic Circle, is one of the 'Seven Summits' - the highest mountains of each of the seven continents, with Mt. Everest at 8848 metres being the highest in the world. Denali is the highest mountain in North America at 6194 metres.

I felt an immediate "Yes" move through me at the prospect of joining this expedition. I was surprised at my full-bodied response because I had never completed an independent expedition of this magnitude, nor altitude before, but it was clear - I must go! At the same time, I had absolutely no idea how I would come close to funding the trip or obtain the necessary specialty gear. I also had a health history of chronic fatigue and while I was fit and capable, I was probably not an obvious athlete for such a serious physical and mental undertaking.

The equipment required to climb Denali is highly technical climbing gear similar to what is needed to climb Mt. Everest. The list includes down-filled suits, plastic boots with moulded thermal inners and neoprene covers, crampons, ice axes, harnesses, ropes, snowshoes, expedition tents, fuel, shovels and high calorie food. With a clear focus, I saved every dollar I could. A friend loaned me her boots, crampons and ice axes and through my connection with an adventure retail store, several companies sponsored me so that I was able to establish the remaining essential high-altitude equipment either via discounted purchase or by generous loan. These offerings were certainly *signs* of support for my adventure.

We planned the trip for summer when there are more than twenty hours of sub-arctic daylight and the temperatures are warmer, maybe *only* -30°C, though the wind-chill factor can make it feel a further 20°C colder again! I flew to Alaska to meet my five Denali friends and from there a tiny plane delivered us onto the Kahiltna Glacier at the base of the mountain. We alighted from the plane into a white sea of snow and ice and piercingly vivid blue sky. We wrangled with our individual 60 kilograms of gear (30-kilogram rucksack + 30-kilogram sled rigged to our harnesses) and roped up in two groups of three - a standard mountaineering safety measure to help mitigate the consequences should one of us fall into a glacial crevasse.

When I am in nature, especially in remote locations involving high exposure, I have noticed that both the clarity and speed of my intuition is heightened. It's very clear to me whom to trust. When an accident or hesitation could likely result in dire consequences, having unwavering trust that your partner completely 'has your back' is essential.

Climbing a high-altitude mountain is logistically complex and relentless. It involves a series of altitude gains, acclimatising (climb high, sleep low), caching gear and food strategically at places up the mountain, and melting snow to make drinking water. Each day was carefully planned to leapfrog our way up the mountain, and some days were spent entirely tent-bound when we were weathered-in by blizzards.

Two weeks in, we arrived at 'Basin Camp' (4330m) and joined another hundred climbers in tents and teams dotted across a relatively flat plateau, surrounded by towering slopes that were prone to avalanche. Most parties make use of five nights sleeping at this altitude to rest, maintain fitness, adjust to the low oxygen conditions, socialise and speculate about the notoriously changeable weather predictions. When the weather patterns appear to be a good fit, teams relocate via a steep 300-meter headwall of snow and ice and a rugged knife edge ridge to 'High Camp' (5245m). After leaving Basin Camp, the ascent conditions change dramatically, and the exposure is considerable. Experienced brothers had died just the day before we started.

Despite the latitude, climate, altitude and terrain being inhospitable and unforgiving, I marvelled at how peaceful I felt on this mountain – I felt so at home. It was an experience of knowing I was exactly where I needed to be – my inner knowing was affirming me again.

On the Basin Camp grapevine, we heard there was to be a window of good weather approaching. A team member, whom I trusted, suggested we make our move to High Camp and then wait a rest day while other mountaineers made their summit bid.

We would bank on good weather for us to summit the following day. I felt a strong intuition that this was the right choice for us, so on our High Camp rest day, we watched everyone head off super early.

The weather that day was the first window clear enough to attempt the hostile summit in weeks. We heard it was very busy on the summit, with a 'traffic jam' situation at the very top where the ridge is narrow with sheer drops thousands of metres down. As the day matured, the weather turned rapidly for the worse, and most climbers were caught out tackling or sheltering from a raging blizzard and whiteout. I was very happy I had trusted my intuition to wait out the extra day.

The next day brought beyond-perfect weather – this is unheard of as mountaintops are notoriously harsh and bitterly unpleasant, no place to 'hang out' and bask in the glow of accomplishment. We ventured off early for the summit on this incredible day, with next to no wind and clear blue sky. Everyone else at High Camp had attempted the summit the day before, so we had the final 1000 metres completely to ourselves! From camp, we initially traversed a treacherous and icy slope (the riskiest and coldest section of the whole expedition) and then persisted slowly, doing our best to cope with low oxygen across varying terrain.

Arriving at the summit felt incredible. Our group had made it, and now could enjoy the summit all to ourselves. It felt like we were literally on top of the world! The vista was breathtakingly phenomenal. Crystal clear skies with a collection of fluffy clouds bobbing far below. The lower peaks of Denali National Park mountain range looked like islands poking out from a sea of clouds.

When climbing a mountain, reaching the top is only half the journey – a 'successful summit' requires a safe descent. Giddy with joy and expansion, we made an unnecessarily fast descent over 36 hours, only to wait three days for the plane to collect us! Fortunately, though, this offered our bodies the dedicated rest we needed to start recovering after our expedition.

After the climb, I reflected and realised that all I needed to do was say "Yes" to that pure passion moving through me and everything then came together for this adventure. Following my intuition throughout the journey resulted in an extraordinary achievement and experience of a lifetime."

It pays to listen to your passion

Sometimes your passion and excitement will speak loudly, as in the example above, and other times you might experience a very subtle sense of excitement. When you are in touch with the varying shades of excitement, they can act as life guidance. It can be in the most refined moment of excitement that you notice an intuitive choice or direction for your path. There is incredible value in attuning to the subtle guidance offered by a twinge of excitement as well as those moments of fully powered exhilaration. You can refer to the practical steps at the end of this chapter for ways to open the communication pathways of your passion and excitement.

Learning curve resistance is normal

Your intuition is always moving you towards more happiness. However, when you choose to follow your excitement, sometimes it may lead you through a learning curve and possibly feelings of resistance. This does not mean that you were off track with your passion or decision to act. Stepping through your resistance can simply be part of the process of allowing in more joy.

For example, you may feel initially passionate about learning guitar and dive into ten lessons. Along the way, there may be some frustrations, such as being awkward while learning, or committing to the time required, or progressing more slowly than desired. Yet by the end of your ten lessons, you would also feel the joy and satisfaction of completing the course and being able to play guitar. At this point, you can choose whether there is enough desire and passion to continue.

As another example, you might feel excited about learning new computer skills and getting involved in online social networking. The ultimate outcome may be to connect with the world in a more joyful and fulfilling way via social media or perhaps by promoting a business venture. However, along the road, you could encounter frustrations in gaining the required skills and understanding the complexities of the social media environment. Resistance may also arise as an intense sense of fear, such as a fear of speaking up and being *seen* on social networks. However, you can choose to follow your initial excitement to reach your goal and step through any frustrations and fears.

Therefore, following your intuition can, and often will, lead you through a process of personal development and learning new skills, while also guiding you to more happiness and fulfilment.

Practical Steps to Embracing Emotional Guidance

You can practice conscious passion, excitement and dreaming of greater outcomes for your life. This is very helpful in opening the pathways to intuition.

1. **Allow yourself enjoyment:** You can align more fully with the channels of intuitive flow by creating greater passion and enjoyment in life through fun, inspiring and rewarding activities and events.

    Write a list of ten favourite activities that uplift you or make you happy, then indulge yourself in some of these on a weekly basis. Make sure you rotate through the items on your list and don't get stuck on the same few. The activities that bring you enjoyment will be unique to you. Here are some examples:
    1. Walks on the beach
    2. Cake and coffee
    3. Movies that uplift you
    4. Meals with friends
    5. Having a massage
    6. Hiking in nature

    Please take time to write *and live* your list – it will pay off. You can use the blank page that follows to create yours.

2. **Allow yourself adventure:** Intuition rides on excitement. You can invite excitement to move through your emotional body by seeking and experiencing adventure. Allow yourself little quests, try new things and factor in some bigger, more challenging adventures along the way. This will open the channels of joy and excitement in your life.

    Tune in to the subtleties of excitement when participating in your adventures. Take time to notice the feeling of enjoyment and excitement moving within you, or call it forward through you so you are consciously aware of the experience. This will build your internal recognition of the feeling of excitement. It will help you to notice when excitement speaks and guides your choices, even in its more subtle form - when there is just a hint of it within you. These glimmers of excitement will act as guidance if you are practiced at being aware of them.

Write a list of ten adventures you would like to experience. Put some time into working out a plan for bringing these experiences into your life. Start with the easiest and most achievable first and continue through the list.

Some examples:

1. Snorkelling in tropical waters
2. Hot-air ballooning
3. Swimming with dolphins
4. Travel plans to *bucket-list* locations
5. Sky diving
6. Climbing a mountain

3. **Track your excitement:** Be open to noticing when you feel passionate or excited about an idea and consider allowing yourself to have or do whatever that may be.

    Some *small-safe-step* examples: Take time out to watch a movie you want to see; spend a day doing something you have wanted to do for ages – it could be as simple as lying on the lounge reading a book for the day, going to an art exhibition, enjoying a particular bush walk, or having a massage or facial.

4. **Review your passion:** If you have committed yourself to a project that you were passionate about initially, and now you are having trouble following through, go back and review what initially triggered your passion. If the passion is still there, consider recommitting to it again with the end

result in mind, or perhaps to a shorter time frame, before you reassess again. Keep in mind that a learning curve and some resistance along the way is natural when following your passion.

5. **Participate in authentic personal development programs or personal counselling:** Find courses and programs that support you to embrace your feelings and emotions in a balanced and healthy manner. Allow your feelings of sadness, joy, anger or love to have a voice. They are communicating a message and are always leading you *home* to the Truth. By giving yourself freedom with your feelings, you clear the pathway of debris, road bumps, and roadblocks to receive your Greater Knowing.

   You will need to use a combination of your intuition and logical discernment to decide which counselling support or personal development programs are best choices for you.

Author's Note: If you are experiencing complex emotional issues or are in a high stress situation or crisis, then you may wish to utilise this information in consultation with your health practitioner or counsellor. When in a time of high stress or crisis, it can be difficult to be in touch with your inner wisdom and you may need to reach out for support. Better to seek support if you are unsure or wait until the dust settles and things calm down before making major life decisions. When you are in a calm place, this is the time to practise the small-safe-steps that help to develop a relationship and familiarity with the language of your intuition.

Please take time to write and live your lists.

Write a list of 10 favourite activities that bring you enjoyment or make you happy.

1. ....

2. ....

3. ....

4. ....

5. ....

6. ....

7. ....

8. ....

9. ....

10. ....

Write a list of 10 adventures you would love to experience.

1. ....

2. ....

3. ....

4. ....

5. ....

6. ....

7. ....

8. ....

9. ....

10. ....

*Your heart speaks to you via love
which is the foundation of your intuition*

4.
Going to the Heart of the Matter

Your heart is part of your inner guidance system. It can move you toward what you want as well as assist you to make your best choices. Your heart speaks to you via love and is the foundation of your intuition. Have you ever said, "I just knew in my heart it was the right thing," or "I'd love to go on that holiday, have that car, or be able to help my friend." Asking yourself the question, "What is in my heart?" can be the best place from which to make decisions. In this way, love is the flow of your heart's desire and can act as inner guidance.

Love exists in every cell of your body, not just in your heart centre. It is the substance of which you are made. Love is how you can *handshake* with the awareness of the Creative Source within your physical body. It allows you to experience a connection with your Greater Knowing within the cells of your body. This means you have the potential to know, within every fibre of your being, as a whole-body experience, the truth about a situation or the direction of guidance you are receiving. The pathway to this depth of knowing is self-love and acceptance.

Self-love

Most people could benefit from a big dose of self-love. Certain life experiences and the negative commentary, or judgement of others, can cause us to shut down from loving ourselves.

A closed heart can block intuition because intuitive ability is founded on an open-hearted receiving of your inner knowing. When you are in a state of self-love, it removes the blocks to intuitive flow and allows your heart to guide you. When you lovingly embrace your feelings, this allows them to move through you and communicate clearly.

Grace - Finances Freed

"My partner and I gained a mortgage to purchase our family home just prior to the unfolding of the Global Financial Crisis. We had reached our borrowing cap because of our modest investment portfolio, thus the interest rate for the loan was at a high 'no documentation rate'. As time passed, we made our regular loan repayments, and the broader economy recovered from the financial crisis. Ultimately, the economic environment changed dramatically, and interest rates slowly declined over the subsequent years to historic lows. We had approached the bank twice during this time to reduce our home loan interest rate in accordance with this decline, but received a solid brick wall response of "No" both times.

During this same decade, we grew our family and had two gorgeous children. We also experienced an income decline due to illness. The combination of lower income and the desire to provide good education and sports lessons for our children placed tremendous pressure on our budget, and we were bending - if not breaking - under the financial strain.

Amidst this financial situation, I had continued actions to support my own personal development and was focused on building my self-esteem, self-love and self-worth. I knew this was a key to increased happiness in my life. I had also been doing a substantial amount of volunteer work for a charity and met many good people through this service. One woman who joined our organisation as a volunteer had a background in investment banking. I felt drawn to ask for her guidance regarding our interest rate situation and how to approach the bank once again. This woman willingly shared her knowledge and explained that after two years of regular repayments, the 'new client' risk to the bank was mitigated, and we were within our rights to receive the standard interest rate. In hindsight, I see the synchronicity of someone with the necessary knowledge arriving in my life at a time when I had developed enough self-worth to ask for help.

Armed with this new knowledge of my rights, I once again wrote a letter to the bank asking for a reduction of our loan rate. The other synchronous event during this time was our banking industry had undergone a Royal Commission into their business practices, resulting in requirements for greater transparency and to act in integrity and fairness with their customers.

Our bank was initially uncooperative. However, with my new level of self-worth on board I was able to stand strong during the negotiations. The outcome, to our delight, was that our interest rate was halved, making a tremendous difference to our monthly budget, freeing up finances and choices for providing for our children."

This story is a wonderful example of how increased self-love can attract in new possibilities, guide us to positive action, and open us to receiving our heart's desire – in this case ease in finances and provision for the family.

Self-love magnetises synchronicities and receiving

The more you love yourself, the more you will allow good things into your life. In fact, the more love you allow through you (love of self), the more you will be *in the flow* of receiving in general. Love is magnetic and will attract toward you the things you desire. In fact, the magnetics around the heart are particularly strong; stronger than the magnetics of your brain.[13] Consider the magnetic power you experience when you are first attracted to someone; it captures your entire being, doesn't it? This is a great reference point for the power of love.

When you are passionately in love with an idea, the magnetic energy of that love can make it easier to manifest in your life as you step forward and follow your heart. This heart-generated magnetic power of attraction can be focused and applied to anything you desire. For example, you may feel you wish to go on a particular holiday. You give it some thought, and your whole body rings with excitement. You literally LOVE the idea!

It's obvious to feel the wisdom of your heart speaking to you in moments like these, isn't it?

Denise - A Holiday for Free

"The company I worked for offered a business incentive with the prize being a trip to Alaska, cruising the stunning Inside Passage. I am typically not fussed about travelling overseas, but absolutely loved the idea of this trip and felt incredibly excited about the possibility. I just knew I was going to be there. I decided to focus on winning the incentive – it was like turning front on to the idea with a clear vision of what I wanted. I made a dream board of the trip, which included a collage of pictures of Alaskan scenery along with a picture of myself right there. I became clear on the business activities that would put me in the running to win the trip. With that focus, things seemed to fall into place for my success. I came across people I could help through my business, and this raised me to a successful outcome of qualifying for the trip.

What an incredible holiday I received – the Alaskan scenery was like sailing through the pages of National Geographic.[14] I loved being in the beauty of nature as we cruised straight up to the faces of enormous ice-blue glaciers and gently sailed past fur seals sunbathing upon floating icebergs. It was a perfect style of holiday for me – a trip of a lifetime and all for free!"

In this story, her heart's desire was ignited by the thought of going on an Alaskan holiday, and her passion for the idea was felt as a whole-body excitement. The magnetic power of love for the idea, combined with some action and envisioning herself there, attracted a series of synchronicities and this potent manifestation into her life.

Stay open to noticing your heart's desire, and then allow yourself to engage in whole-body excitement about the idea you love. (Refer back to the practical steps on allowing pleasure and excitement in Chapter 3, if you need further help.) This combination, together with taking some action, is a powerful way to manifest your desires. The truth is that manifestation is founded on loving yourself enough to allow yourself to hear and follow your heart's desire.

Self-love combined with intent can reconfigure your life experience

Increasing self-love can improve the way you experience your relationships as well as your relationship with life in general. Once you identify something you want in your heart, you can utilise your intention to move you toward that desire. In this way, your intuitive heart's desire will guide you toward life improvement.

Amie - Love Leads the Way

"I was experiencing a difficult relationship with a work colleague for several years. I had been at the receiving end of distrust and unkindness, which was a constant source of upset for me. Over a Christmas holiday break, I was contemplating what I wanted to achieve for the year ahead and decided one of the things I desired was an easier, more peaceful and kinder relationship with this person. Around the same time, the concept of practicing self-love had been reignited within me and I was choosing to spend time on a regular basis sending love to myself. Initially, choosing to love myself, and also focusing on having a more loving experience with someone else, appeared to be separate life choices to me.

As the year progressed, I noticed my colleague began being more open and kinder toward me, even acknowledging and thanking me for the work that I had been doing. This was a significant and noticeable shift in our relating and I was marvelling at the change. I started to contemplate what had happened for me to experience this. It took me a while to put two and two together, and then it struck me – I believe that practising self-love and appreciation had created a dynamic positive shift in the relationship with my work colleague. It had not occurred to me previously that making a choice for more self-love might be the key to allowing more love and kindness to flow towards me from someone else."

In Amie's story, she gave intent to her heart's desire to improve her work relationship, even though she did not know how it might happen. She was also motivated (a sign of inner guidance) during this same time to focus on self-love. Though not necessarily consciously linking her intent with the desire for increasing self-love, they formed a powerful combination that resulted in a significant positive change in that relationship.

You could be motivated by your heart's desire to improve many aspects of your life; relationships, family, work and career, your physical health, spirituality or creativity. Each desire is intuitively guiding you to experience something better in life. Embodying a deeper sense of self-love and self-worth will allow the motivations of your heart to move through you because you know you are worthy of those desires. Self-love will also provide the base of self-esteem and confidence to know you can make these improvements in your life through utilising your intention and taking some action.

The path of integrity

Choosing to follow your heart is a path of integrity. Not just integrity within your choices (though it definitely will drive authentic choices), but the choice for heart-based integrity will also influence the meld and flow of your life. If you could imagine your life as a fluid process, then this fluid substance will be moulded and formed by the presence of love into the greatest outcome for you. Choosing to act with heart-based integrity also positions you as a receiver of this high vibration in your life. When you include love and integrity in your decision-making process, the outcomes are more likely to be for your highest good and the highest good of those affected by your choices.

Lisa - Integrity in Career Choices

"I had travelled back to my home state for a work conference. While I was there, I visited the state organisation for the services in my industry. During the visit, I had a strong experience of knowing in my bones that being the head of this state organisation was the job I would have in the future.

Five years later, I moved back to my home state and worked in regular services within my industry. I ended up in a work situation with a fantastic salary and many benefits, including a car. Then a position came up for the Head of the State business organisation – the position five years earlier I had felt drawn to. I absolutely knew I had to go for it. I aspired to a new vision of that business and the organisation as a whole, and I knew I was the right person for the job. The business had been floundering, lost its funding, was experiencing significantly reduced staff numbers and a challenging relationship with the membership.

The career move meant a drop of $50,000 in my yearly salary and sacrificing all the benefits I had in my current position. However, I knew the only choice of integrity was to follow my knowing that this was the right choice – it had purpose in it.

I went into that organisation and was able to turn it around and grow the business. Relationships were built, old grievances were laid to rest and common purpose was identified and strengthened. We started to receive grants, founded a training organisation, and legitimised our industry. Five years later, we had grown the membership by over ninety percent, the staff had grown tenfold, government consulted with us, and we were financially in a position to move forward. We were united and stood with one voice.

The core of my business plan was to build a 'business with heart' – firmly bedded in building relationships, transparent business practices, valuing people by word and actions and shared decision-making. Our core value was an unwavering delivery of quality services to our community. All staff were responsible to our core values, and those not aligned to these values left the organisation.

When I retired from the position, I left knowing the contribution I made to the industry, and the leadership I provided, was valued and had made a difference. At the time of my departure, I felt the business required a new level of business skills. Luckily, the person who could offer this expertise was already working within the organisation and continued to take it from strength to strength."

The power of the heart

The more you are connected in your heart (via love) with someone, the more in tune you will be with them - this could mean anyone you feel open-hearted towards. Love creates a strong, empathic line of communication between people that is virtually instantaneous. This type of connection is evident in stories where someone has a sense that a friend or family member is in trouble or needs help.

Often, in retrospect, you will see an obvious benevolent aspect within a knowing that emanated from your heart and involved the message of loving care.

Joy - Taking Care of Mum

"I use my intuition frequently to guide care for my mother, who is ageing and dealing with progressing dementia. She lives a long distance away, so I manage her health and general care long distance and visit in person when I can. It's amazing what can be done with the phone and internet these days. I have learned to trust my feelings when I experience an impulse to phone or check with Mum, even if I have just spoken with her that morning or perhaps the day before. Upon calling her again, I have often discovered an urgent situation that needs handling or simply her need to talk about something. It is as if I have an inbuilt radar when it comes to her."

Heather - Father in Distress

"My 89-year-old father, who lives alone, had been using a chemotherapy cream on his face for skin cancers. I had a bad feeling about him using it and suspected he would find the effects distressing. My brother phoned to say Dad's face was swollen, and we agreed to tell him to stop using the cream. Thoughts of my father were still going through my mind days later, so I phoned to check on him. He was feeling depressed about his face, which had been bleeding, and this had spiralled him into such a low emotional state he had stayed indoors all day. I was able to reassure him, we chatted for a while, had some laughs, and he was much better by the time we finished the phone call."

Janis - Best Friends

"I have a close girlfriend of over 40 years. We have experienced long gaps in contact over the years, and we don't speak that frequently as we live in different parts of the country and have quite separate lives now, but she remains in my heart. We have had a dynamic between us our entire lives where we know when we are thinking of each other and possibly need to speak. Whenever we do make contact, we discover that indeed we have both been thinking of each other."

Melanie - Conscious Communication

"A friend was strongly on my mind, to the extent it felt uncanny, so I texted her to say I had been thinking of her and maybe it was time to catch-up. She replied later that day to say she had been doing a 'mindful marathon' which included a run, yoga and meditation, and had been thinking of me!"

In each of these examples, a heart-based relationship was the foundation for receiving personal guidance for connection and delivery of benevolent, loving care.

Mother's intuition

As the provider of care for her children, a mother's brain is especially tuned for the intuitive process. Undoubtedly, the intuitive ability of a mother is intensified by the power of love for her child.

Lesley - Mother's Intuition

"I have three children, all currently under ten years old. I had my first child when I was 32 and I noticed a difference within me on becoming a first-time mum. Motherhood had awakened a knowing of something deeper inside, particularly with regard to intuitive care for my child. Despite all the parenting advice from books, people and medical experts, I felt that nothing provided deep or satisfying answers to my parenting questions.

My first baby was upset most of the time during the first few months. This resulted in me being severely sleep deprived, so I went to the doctor to seek advice. The doctor told me that this was "Just mothering and what babies do." I left the appointment with a strong sense of dissatisfaction and felt a resistance in me that said, "No, my baby wouldn't be crying like this if nothing was wrong." At that point, I realised that doctors don't hold all the knowing and felt I had the ability to know what was best for my children. I started to act more on this sense of knowing within me. I began to explore complementary and natural dietary choices, and I discovered some adjustments in breast feeding and supplemental milk that made a difference. Over a much longer period of time, I realised that my daughter's upset was sometimes a response to my own stress. I also discovered she needed the balancing effect of nature more than I did. Whenever she was unsettled, taking her out into nature would bring her more balance. I noticed that nature would seem to *speak* to me and remind me to bring this balance in for her. There have been many occasions where a bird would fly into my view, or make itself known to me in some way, and this became my reminder to take her out into nature.

My intuitive knowing continued to develop over time as I trusted myself and experienced the positive outcomes of decisions I made for my child. I also found that my intuition expanded and deepened with the arrival of each of my children.

By the time my second daughter arrived, I felt *I know how to do this* and didn't need to know what everyone else was saying or thinking. I felt those opinions had no relevance to me and my baby because they did not meet the individual relationship I had with my child. Knowing this, I connected with my daughter very quickly - I could see she sensed my certainty - I wasn't questioning myself.

In the journey with my intuition, I discovered each child had their own qualities, which led me to explore the breadth of my inner knowing and feel out what was right for them as individuals.

When I was 12 weeks pregnant with my third child, my husband passed away suddenly. Apart from the grieving process, this left me with many sole parenting decisions for my children. As the birth approached, I was feeling frustrated and nervous about being on my own in having to make the decision for our baby's name. I felt it was a particularly important one, with many people interested in my decision. I had been having *discussions* at night with my husband and Spirit, calling in some guidance for a name. Without knowing the gender of my baby, I had started writing a list of names for boys and girls. About three weeks before the birth, I woke at three in the morning, and the name *Theo* came to me. I got out of bed and wrote it down, as I felt it was a message.

By this stage, I felt my intuition had developed to a whole other level of knowing what was right for me and my child for this birth. I arranged the support of a birthing partner and a midwife of my choice. I also organised to have my baby in a hospital birthing room to provide a backdrop of safety around the birth. I then planned to follow the birth with three days to simply be and bond with my baby, before returning home to also care for my two daughters.

Not all my family agreed with this idea of three days of individual time with my new child, but I knew it was right for me and my newborn. I knew the pressures of childbirth and the need for some recovery time. After my son was born, we packed up and went to the place I had arranged, where my parents also stayed to care for us. My newborn son and I just slept and fed together – both of us. During this time, I sat with the name I had felt guided for him - Theo. After three days, I was sure it was right for him.

At a time when both my parents, and my husband's parents were all together, I told them the name I had decided for my newborn child. I saw my husband's father become teary, and his mother asked me, "Do you know?" I shook my head because I didn't know what she meant. She told me that *Theo* was the name of my husband's first sailing boat, which had been a deep love and passion for him."

Self-worth is a major key

A major factor influencing intuitive flow is your level of self-worth; a high level of self-worth means valuing your knowing and your *self*. (When I use the term 'your *self*', I'm speaking of your true inner essence or core *self*, that which encompasses the greatness of your soul and bears witness to your life.) Developing self-worth is about improving the relationship you have with the truth of who you are, and the beauty and wisdom held within you. Focusing on raising your sense of self-worth and improving your self-love and self-acceptance is critical to hearing, trusting and following your feelings and inner knowing. A strong sense of self-worth positions you to fully receive your inner guidance.

Self-love means making it your business to consciously choose to love and accept your self despite circumstances. To love your self for the very essence of who you are without referencing anything material in your life. It means choosing to extend kindness and compassion to your self. It can also be helpful to acknowledge what's good about your self and your life, to fully receive the value of who you are as an individual. Increasing your level of self-worth requires your time and focus. This vital work will underpin your ability to trust your creative flow and inspirations.

Many people have had the experience of their ideas and creativity being squashed, either during childhood, schooling or working life. As a result, they may not honour the inspired ideas that move through them as guidance. In fact, many people talk themselves out of their inspired ideas.

This influence can result in not trusting your inner wisdom when it speaks. It is important to understand that your inner wisdom has nothing to do with intellect and everything to do with your unique creative internal process.

The more you lovingly embrace your current circumstances and feelings, and the more love you allow in, the clearer the lines of communication are going to be with your inner knowing.

Practical Steps to Integrate Conscious Receiving

Practising *conscious receiving* is a wonderful pathway to open your intuitive flow.

Some exercises outlined below may be familiar to you. Apart from developing your connection to self, they also deepen the receiving of your intuition. The key to their success is to practise them on a daily or regular basis.

There are four aspects of conscious receiving that will assist you in receiving deeper intuition:

1. Receiving your self
2. Receiving life
3. Receiving your intuition
4. Receiving your spiritual connection

1. Receiving your self

Practicing self-love and appreciation on a daily basis increases happiness, life satisfaction, and attracts even more into your life to appreciate.

- **Take time daily to focus on loving appreciation of your self.** This could be done any time but is most beneficial when you make it a regular habit. A good time to practice can be just as you turn off the light to go to sleep or as soon as you wake-up in the morning. These can be powerful moments, as you drift in or out of a subconscious state, to set the focus of your mind on sending love to your self or in self-appreciation. This may feel like you are pretending or imagining the flow of love initially, but after regular practice, you will actually shift to feeling the presence of love in the cells of your body.

  This process helps move self-love from a concept of the mind to integrating self-love as a whole-body experience.

- **Written self-love exercise** – this is most effectively done with pen and paper and will focus your awareness on self-love and appreciation.

  Write at the top of the page: *Something I love and appreciate about myself is...*

  Take the time to write a list of three to five items for each of the following categories.

  Physical – e.g., legs, hair, nails, face, figure

  Intellectual – e.g., ability to plan, intelligence, fun loving

  Spiritual – e.g., connection with nature and animals, compassion for others, community values

  Personal qualities – e.g., kindness, integrity, compassion, contribution, good listener

  God-given talents – e.g., musical, creativity, sports talents, cooking

- **Using self-worth affirmations** – "I am worthy" or "I am lovable." Say your affirmation out loud, tune into your body and say it as if speaking from the cells of your body. Consciously choosing to mean it and believe it as true, as you express them, will give these affirmations strength and power.

- **Participate in processes that increase self-love and self-worth** – such as self-development programs, lovingly giving to yourself, allowing yourself to receive compliments, increasing physical self-care or forgiving yourself. These will open the flow of receiving within you, including the receiving of your intuition.

2. Receiving your life

Practicing appreciation and gratitude builds a field of attraction for receiving.

Spend at least a few minutes a day focusing on appreciation and gratitude. Practicing gratitude engenders greater love of life, joy, passion, and the flow of your intuition.

What are you grateful for today? You could speak this aloud or write it down in a journal.

Be grateful for the simple things right through to the more significant experiences in your life. Some examples - I am grateful for the rain watering my garden, the sun on my body when out for a walk, the extra money I unexpectedly received yesterday, my children making me laugh, my chiropractor taking care of my body, spending time with my friends, or my work that provides an income.

Immerse yourself in the *feeling* of gratitude. Sometimes it may feel as if you are simply saying or writing words with little or no authenticity. However, as you practice, there will be times when gratitude will flow naturally and fully through you. What a wonderful, joyous feeling that is! As you choose to regularly focus on being grateful, you will find spontaneous moments of gratitude will become more frequent. In turn, you will live increasingly with a sense of satisfaction in your life.

Appreciation exercise - practice this daily for seven days. You can either journal it or say it aloud. The purpose is to establish gratitude as a routine.

Write down or speak out gratitude for the following:

- 5 big things you are experiencing in your life

- 5 little things you are experiencing in your life

I have included some blank pages at the end of this chapter for gratitude journaling.

3. Receiving your intuition

Be grateful to your intuition directly. This is an exercise in acknowledging your intuition when it speaks to you.

When you notice your intuition guiding you, stop, take note, and thank it in the moment. If you notice synchronicity in your life, stop, take note and say, "Thank you." If you receive a flash of a vision that gives you direction in life, stop, take note, and smile to yourself. These are some of the wonderful aspects of your intuition appearing in your life.

Please see further exercises in Chapter 6, 'The Voice of Your Intuition', where there are more activities on receiving and amplifying your intuition.

4. Receiving your connection to your Higher Self / God / Creative Source

Each person has a unique understanding of and relationship with a Greater Power in their life, which guides and supports them. Whatever your belief about this Source, there are benefits to choosing to consciously connect with it and welcome this loving support into your life. The energy of Creative Source exists within and around you always, and with focus you can open your channels of awareness to this ever-present, loving energy.

Gently focus on sending love to your Higher Self and be open to receiving a sense of connection with the ALL-benevolent, loving presence that is there for you. Again, this may start as simply imagining without any real sense of connection, but it will evolve into a deeper connection if you stay with the process. You can allow this practice to mature into a full-body experience of the love that exists around and within you. Once you experience this, you will know in your heart the loving presence that is eternally with you and constantly emanating pure love to you, and there will be no turning back.

Please also see Chapter 10, 'Spiritual Assistance', for more exercises on receiving the power of love and support from Divine Source.

In summary

Have you noticed the theme of these practical exercises?

They are all about establishing a loving relationship with your self, your life, and your Creative Source. Consciously opening the channels of receiving in your life opens the pathway for profound intuitive flow to communicate through you and be fully received by you. Try these practices, and you will experience your intuition expand and deepen.

Gratitude Journal for Seven Days

Examples:

The birds I hear when I wake up in the morning.

The rain filling my water tanks.

The gift of flowers from my neighbour.

The walk I had on the beach over the weekend.

Where I live amongst nature.

The wonderful massage I had last week.

A lovely luncheon with friends yesterday.

The wonderful sauna I had this week.

The local farmers who supply my fruit and veges at my town market.

My dog's loving presence.

Gratitude Journal for Seven Days

Gratitude Journal for Seven Days

You are connected to a greater
stream of knowing
that is motivating you toward
your highest good.

5.
Small Steps Lead to Leaps of Faith

It is rare for people to be comfortable taking a big leap of faith in their intuition when they first start out. It is usually a step-by-step, day-by-day process of building trust and a relationship with your inner knowing. This is normal, natural and builds your intuition foundation over time.

Even if an angel appeared in its full glory and gave you a message today, you would most likely experience fear in response to such an event, followed by a personal process of trusting yourself in following that message.

Angelic sightings, though they do still happen, are much less likely these days because, as we evolve, it is more helpful for us to learn to become *sovereign* to ourselves. This means learning to trust and follow your own knowing rather than looking to an outside source for guidance. A direct connection to your Greater Knowing is more available now than at any other time during human evolution, and it is your task to open to this connection.

So, let's get down to the small-safe-steps. Building trust in the small things allows you to take bigger leaps of faith as you progress. Remember, the faith is in your self (not in some outside source) and in the fact that you are connected to a greater stream of knowing; a knowing which is motivating you toward your highest good.

Are you listening?

Listening is the key. If someone shows that they are listening to you, doesn't that make you feel respected and valued? How does it build your connection with that person? Does it make you feel appreciation and gratitude? It's the same with building a relationship with your intuition. Your intuition is your best friend and will respond to your listening. Are you keeping tuned and responsive to those subtle messages moving through you by listening to your intuition?

Here are a couple of examples of small-safe-steps you can take to develop your intuitive listening.

1. You are driving to a regular destination and notice an inclination to travel via a different route. Do it. No harm done. You may never know why it was a better choice to change your course; however, you are now choosing to trust and follow an intuitive feeling as it moves through you. You may discover later that there was a major roadblock along your usual route. Or it could be that you simply felt happier taking the other path. Either way, it's a great outcome. By trusting this inner call and taking action, you are building a relationship with your intuition by saying, "*I am listening to you.*"

2. Perhaps you have a huge work agenda for the day. Logic says you should sit down and work, but you notice a deep desire within you to go for a walk in the sun. Your mind might say, "*I need to keep working.*" Yet your heart says, "*The sun is calling me.*" You choose to take a walk. While out in the sun, you relax, and some ideas begin to flow on a project you have been stuck on, or you think of a shortcut to get through your agenda, or the walk revives your energy in a way that helps you return to your work and finish it happily in half the time. In this way, listening to and following your intuition can lead to a more efficient outcome.

Some might wonder if this choice to go for a walk, rather than work, could simply be a life pattern of procrastination. If you know you are a procrastinator, then this dynamic may play out in your life, but there is a difference in the energy of intuition and procrastination. There is more information on intuition versus life patterns in Chapter 8 and this will help you with how to distinguish between them and your inner guidance. Through trial and experience in small-safe-steps you will learn to distinguish your intuition from the influence of your life patterns. This example is a small-safe-step based on your heart's desire to go out in nature for a walk, and the outcome in this case was clarity and ease of thought, validating intuition. If it had resulted in more delay, then procrastination may have been driving the desire.

Your intuition is always moving you towards more ease, flow and purpose in your life, and small-safe-steps is a great way to explore and align with that flow.

Slowing down

*Hearing y*our intuition often requires practise at slowing down, connecting with your self and taking time to tune in. It's rare to feel in touch with your intuition when you are in a stressed and rushed phase of life. If you are stressed, you will most likely end up feeling disconnected and out of tune. Remember, intuition speaks through feelings, and feelings have a slower vibrational pace than thoughts. Taking a slower, calmer approach can assist you in being more present with how you feel and what you want and allow the space for inspired thought.

Sometimes you may be forced to slow down due to exhaustion, illness or even because of an emotional upset, such as having a much-needed cry or an episode of anger. Have you noticed that when you recover from an upset, you feel calmer and more settled? This is because moving your feelings also changes your vibration, and this allows for a new perspective.

Life can move at a frenetic pace in the modern world, with an incredible amount of input and information overload on a daily basis. Sometimes you may find that is simply the way of things for a particular phase of your life during which goals are achieved, or projects are handled. However, it will serve you to seek balance and also have regular time for slowing down, rest and inner focus. Slowing down will assist you in feeling calmer and clearer on the subject at hand.

Jenny - Rest Brings Inspired Action

"I was on holidays and having an extra-long sleep after an exhausting work agenda over the previous months. While resting in bed and playing on my iPad, a friend sent me a link to a video. Normally, I wouldn't watch social media clips because I don't have time, but this timing was perfect. I watched the video, which led me to get out a book I hadn't read for some time. I read the whole book and by that afternoon had created a new vision board, written a new meal plan and taken steps towards becoming healthier. This is something I always put off because I've been too busy. It all just *felt right* and has been really easy to follow and stay on track with. Slowing down, right timing and following my intuition led me to take action and make much needed changes."

Alison - Rest Brings Clarity

"It was a long weekend, and I was taking a slower pace on life. The previous three months had been incredibly busy for me. I decided to lie on the lounge for a while, and as I lay there, I was reflecting on all I had achieved in that time and received a clear intuition that I had just finished a cycle of some kind – it felt significant. I then received a strong feeling to take a breather for some time before going forward. Later that same weekend, I was driving to visit some friends and happened to see a sign that said, *"Take a moment."* I knew this was validation of my earlier intuition."

Elizabeth - A Call to Balance

"I had experienced a phase where it had been *all work and no play*. I started to feel a bit miserable and conscious of feeling stuck in a pattern of overwork and needing to find balance. Lo and behold, a local newspaper had erected a huge roadside advertisement, which I drove past several times a week, that said in enormous letters, "RELAX, ENJOY, UNWIND." (The billboard included images of people relaxing and holding their newspapers.) That sign felt like it spoke very loudly to me to make this a priority and drew my attention every time I drove by. That was enough of a message for me - I immediately took action to factor in more play and relaxation in my life."

Leaps of faith

As you build trust and develop a relationship with your intuitive messages, taking a leap of faith in following your inner guidance will become easier, and in some ways, it will seem an obvious choice. Some choices may even have a sense of risk about them, yet you know it is the only choice to make, and what exists on the other side is usually something better for you.

Leaps of faith are unique to each individual. A leap of faith choice for someone could be an easy step for another – it is important not to judge yourself or compare yourself to others as you move through your individual process.

Tracey - Choosing a Pet

"I was devastated when my beloved 12-year-old dog passed away. During the grieving period, I felt strongly that I wanted another dog. I decided to start looking for a rescue dog. A friend had suggested this, and the idea stood out to me. So, I did some exploration online and found a few options. I enquired about and subsequently visited a dog at a nearby refuge, but he just didn't feel right at all.

Ongoing exploration led me to another local animal shelter website. Among the pictures of many dogs, I was drawn to a grey fluffy Shih-Tzu. His little face appealed to me. On the Saturday morning, I felt a strong desire to visit and see him, so phoned to make arrangements.

As soon as I met him, with his soft curly hair, little pushed-in nose, and sweet wiggle of a walk, I had the thought he was the right one. He came straight up to me and rolled over on his back – very cute! Even as I played with him, my mind raised various doubts. I decided to give myself some time over the weekend, trusting that if he was the right dog for me, then he would still be available. The following Tuesday, it so happened I had the rare opportunity to travel out during my workday to visit the shelter and see him again. The woman in charge there gave me some time with him in a private enclosure. He just laid there, patiently waiting for me to get it.

It felt like a big decision for me - it could be a 15-year commitment after all, and I was still recovering from my loss. Despite my fears and resistance, he still felt like *my* dog, so I decided to take a leap of faith and adopt him. When I picked him up a few days later, I felt nauseous in my stomach, which didn't feel like calm intuition to me at all! I knew, however, this was most likely just my fear of commitment and loss churning my stomach. He turned out to be the most gorgeous, faithful, calm, loving presence – a true light in my life. I could not have designed a better little companion dog for myself."

Janet - Career Leap

"I had been working in the film industry for 25 years. On the last film, some expectations of mine were not being met - there was insufficient challenge for me, and I started feeling restless. I felt I was not in the right place anymore and became irritable and moody. I knew something was shifting inside me but didn't understand what it was about.

The turning point happened when my production designer, who liked my work, invited me to join a project in America. It was then I realised I had no fire in the belly for it, the passion had gone. This was a strong sign for me to move on.

At the same time, I had a growing feeling I wanted to be more in control of my finances. This was following the recent discovery I was being underpaid for the same work as the men in my industry.

I left the project I was on, and it was with a sense of elation I drove up the highway, having no idea of my work prospects or how I was going to earn an income. However, I knew I would never work in the film industry again. I felt liberated this shift had happened – I knew I couldn't stay the same and had to move forward.

Although I felt very frightened, I knew something was ahead

of me. About a month after returning to my hometown, an old friend contacted me and introduced me to a series of financial investment seminars on wealth creation. He became my first guide in what was to become my new career as a Financial and Property Investor and I've never looked back. This has been a fulfilling and successful career change for me, and my passion is to use property development as a way to fund my other projects of interest."

Sandra - Trusting Inspired Ideas Fulfils a Purpose

"I had befriended a local family on my many visits to India. The mother's youngest child had just started school, and as her children were no longer the primary focus of her life, I asked about her goals and what she wanted to do next.

I had a deep sense of wanting to help her. After many conversations and over many months discussing her options, she came up with the idea of tending some water buffalo. As an illiterate woman, the work she understands best is how to care for farm animals. The buffalo would provide milk for her family and give her status in the village.

A friend of mine highlighted to me how small that goal was compared to our goals in a western developed country. I had the inspired idea to assist my Indian friend to develop her interest into a small business, so that she could employ other women in the village and, in so doing, improve their lives as well.

I started to spread the word among my friends back home. We arranged a loan to get the project started. This was a leap of faith in my idea, as I had no experience setting up a charity. My women friends entrusted me with the project and their donated funds.

The Buffalo Project now gives a group of Indian women some financial independence from their husbands. They use the proceeds to educate their children and provide milk for their families. They even make dung cakes from the buffalo droppings, which are sold as fuel supply.

It took this project a year to pay back the initial cost of three cows, and this was reinvested into an expanded cow shelter. Profits were used for the women to buy generators for their homes because the electricity supply in the area is unreliable and they are often without power.

Due to illiteracy, none of the Indian women involved were able to manage the project, so I have handled this remotely. However, one of the women's daughters, who has had the benefit of a school education, is able to keep the accounting books under my guidance. This role has now inspired this young woman to become an accountant."

Messages might keep repeating

Intuition will keep repeating the same message if you don't *hear* it the first time. Your task is to listen and act. It may keep approaching you from a variety of angles if you are open to recognising them.

Denise - Guidance for Health

"I had been troubled for a long time with a gut infection and a range of very uncomfortable digestive symptoms. After several years, it became apparent that it may be more serious than I realised. I later discovered I was carrying an infection as a result of a tick bite I had received ten years earlier.

Even though I had been trying many natural therapies, my condition was becoming progressively worse. I was committed to using natural therapies but had heard of many people receiving good results using long-term antibiotics and other drugs. I had serious concern of the damage this kind of treatment might do to my digestive health. I remained resistant to taking pharmaceutical medication, particularly long-term. I started seeing a local doctor, who specialised in this area of health, and he also suggested long-term antibiotics was the best treatment.

I resisted antibiotic treatment for a further twelve months, despite waking a few times, either in the middle of the night or first thing in the morning, feeling unwell and with the thought I needed antibiotics. At this time, I started to hear and read about the concept of 'Integrative Health'. This concept emphasises the benefits of using complementary healthcare alongside Western medicine. I had a gut feeling from these repeated messages that I was being guided to embrace Western medicine into my extensive health regime.

Launching into a long-term antibiotic regime was a leap of faith for me. I put my fears aside and went ahead with the treatment. The result was my health improved significantly over a 6 to 18-month period. This was not the final answer to my recovery, but it did provide a timely pathway out of a significantly depleted health situation. Upon reflection, I can see my fear-based resistance to the many messages I received over time that antibiotics might be a good choice. I am glad I finally trusted the signs."

Jade - A Pregnancy Success Story

"I was using IVF to fall pregnant and had originally narrowed the sperm donor options down to three candidates, based on their answers to the questionnaire they completed when donating sperm. I continued to have trouble falling pregnant over a 12-month period and kept receiving a variety of messages that appeared to be saying the donor wasn't the right one, even though on paper he had the most alignment with the characteristics we felt were appropriate.

The first sign that made me question my choice of donor was a dream that indicated there was a block to receiving a child from this person. The second prompt was more straight-forward – the IVF support program suggested changing donors. Together, these signs were enough to prompt me to select another donor from our other two options. This time, the choice was based on my favourite numbers, which I matched with the donor's allocated identification number. I subsequently fell pregnant immediately. We were blessed with a beautiful son and then two years later gorgeous twins, a boy and a girl."

Both these stories are good examples of intuition attempting to gain attention from a variety of angles over a period of time and, in these cases, to support personal leaps of faith.

Push on the door[15]

Sometimes we have an idea but feel unsure whether it is our best course of action, good timing, or even possible to realise. Rather than allowing self-doubt to get in the way, it can be worthwhile to explore your inspiration by taking some form of action and watching what unfolds. This can be thought of as literally *pushing on the door* of your idea to observe if it swings open and clears the way toward your desire.

However, if your actions do not appear to result in any progress, it may not necessarily be time to completely ditch your idea. You can try again later if you find yourself inspired afresh, as it could be better timing for your circumstances to fall into place at this future point.

A gentle push on a door may open it just enough for you to see the next step forward. By taking a step towards a choice, you can see if the door opens, and things seem to flow in this new direction. Any subsequent flow is a wonderful affirmation of your intuition and an indication of good timing. This is the power of following those gentle nudges from your intuition.

Nora - Dancing and Much More

"I was feeling like I wanted to go back to dance classes but reluctant to travel too far at night. I decided to research what was available locally (I pushed on the door of the idea) and found there was a dance class ten minutes' drive away at a local hall. I chose to try the class out for three sessions (I pushed on the door a bit more) and found it was perfect for my needs. It was a great community of people, and I built a lovely friendship with my teachers, which were both unexpected and delightful outcomes from my original motivation to have fun dancing."

Emily - Push on the Property Door

"My wife owned equal share in a residential property with her previous partner. Relations were tenuous in this previous relationship, so she was wanting to sell her portion to invest elsewhere. Our friends were also saying it might be a good idea for her to move on. However, I just knew and felt strongly my wife should hold her position and possibly even buy out the other share but had no idea how she might go about negotiating this within this strained relationship situation.

We sat with the idea for a while. Down the track, her previous partner wanted to move away from the area, and I felt this was right timing to suggest we buy out her share. She was not only open to the idea, the door swung wide open and she happily sold her share to us. We approached our bank for a loan to cover the cost and the whole process flowed very easily.

We had no plans to sell the house at any particular time in the future. However, over the ensuing 12 months, property prices skyrocketed in the area. Again, I just knew and felt very strongly we should sell on the upswing of the market. We approached our local real estate agent, who decided to hold an open home even before all the marketing material had been finalised. The first person who viewed the house put in a bid, and then amazingly, up-bid on the property, and it was sold by the end of the day. We made a profit of 30 percent in 12 months and were able to use those funds to pay down the mortgage on our own home. I'm very happy I trusted my intuition on timing and pushed on the doors to make it happen."

At times, you might have to push on a few different doors regarding your idea to see which one opens. This may in fact lead you to something even better than your original idea.

Ivy - Accommodation Needed

"My teenage daughter and I needed to move from a long-term, comfortable living situation. We had established shared accommodation that was adequate but not very supportive. This led me to crave a home space surrounded with my own furniture and possessions, and one that was close to my daughter's new school, as she was transitioning to high school in the New Year.

I applied for a beautiful rental home I thought was perfect, but because of a series of delays and maintenance renovations, we had to move to 'temporary' accommodation with a couple of my girlfriends. In the end, the rental I had applied for fell through and we were left to stay with my friends and keep looking.

The New Year began, and my daughter made the leap to high school. I noticed I had no impetus to make a move, or in fact, even look to see what was available. As time passed, I started to question why I wasn't in action to establish our new home, but there was no motivation to move within me at all.

At the same time, I had been having problems with a uterine prolapse which, despite trialling the best natural methods, was becoming worse. My doctor referred me for a hysterectomy, and at this point I knew this was the best choice for me. With my previous resistance to surgery falling away, I was placed on a public waiting list for the operation.

The year was ticking by, and my daughter was settling into high school and our temporary home. I was increasingly finding our share situation to be very supportive to her wellbeing, being surrounded by a small tribe of very supportive women at home. They assisted with her homework and transported her around, and it was giving me much needed relief from the challenges of bringing up a teenager. I found myself living in a household that was honouring, very supportive, and one where we could relax. A wonderful flow had developed between us all.

My operation date arrived, and I was informed the recovery period would be six weeks, including the first two weeks largely in bed! My housemates and friends circled around and took care of me and my daughter. I could not have designed a better recovery situation where I was able to relax and let go. Both my daughter and I were cared for beautifully.

As I look back on this situation, I can see the perfection of living with my friends. Although I had originally desired my own independent living situation, what unfolded was something much, much better."

This is a wonderful story of pushing on a door that did not open (attempting to move into an independent dwelling) because there was a better outcome to unfold - being surrounded by a tribe of women who supported her with health and family.

Your pathway is unique

You will be guided along your own unique and rewarding life path by your intuition.

Your life choices may not necessarily be the best ones for another person in a similar situation. There are infinite possibilities in each life scenario, and your intuition can wisely guide you through the maze of choices. It could indeed be that someone else's answer gives you clues to yours, but it is important that you follow the signs intuitively for your individual course of action.

This knowing will come via a *special resonance or feeling tone* that you recognise within yourself around the message. There is more on the tonality of your intuition and recognising the unique voice of your intuition in the next chapter.

Start with safe steps

Learning with small-safe-steps is the best pathway to taking those leaps of faith. Only you will know when the timing is right to take your personal leaps of faith.

Practical Ways to Take Small-safe-steps

1. **Talk to your intuitive aspect**. You can establish a feedback loop with your intuition. Make your conscious mind your friend by asking your intuition *out loud* to make you aware when it is sending you messages.

    You will likely start to notice when your intuition *speaks* to you. Recognition of the message is based in the *feeling* you experience, as it will stand out to you in some way. Be willing to listen to that part of yourself and play with it in small-safe-steps.

    When you think your intuition is guiding you and it *feels right*, back it up with a small action. For example, go shopping somewhere different if you feel the urge to do so, give that friend a call if you keep thinking about them, or choose not to do something if you feel resistant to it (e.g., staying at home when you don't feel like going out).

2. **Practice trusting.** Don't try to figure out or look for validation for why you were moved in a certain way. It may never be obvious to you, or it may become obvious at a later date. Either way, it's not a competition. It's a process of opening the pathways to your inner knowing. Simply choose to trust the process and your choices, and start with small-safe-steps.

3. **Ask for the messages to repeat.** Your intuition is gentle and patient and will repeat messages if you are open to them. If you are not clear about the guidance you receive, you can ask for messages to be repeated. This can be particularly useful for gaining clarity. Guidance can be multi-faceted, so making a conscious request for a repeat can provide the chance for a further affirmation. It may repeat, through a variety of messages and from different angles, as in the pregnancy success and guidance for health stories in this chapter.

4. **Push on the door.** If you think you are being guided toward certain choices, *push on the door* and see what happens. The

concept of pushing the door combines intuition with the idea of taking small-safe-steps and a willingness to observe the results. It is a good way of moving forward to explore what evolves.

Slow down, be present and tune-in

1. **Meditation** is not for everyone but can be a wonderful way to connect with your self and your greater knowing. It will centre you and calm your mind.

   There are many forms of meditation, and you may like to explore different techniques until you find the one that best suits you. Once you become familiar with the general process, you may choose to utilise different methods as the mood takes you such as:

   - Use a mantra by repeating a key word in your mind.
   - Try a guided meditation or visualise something you wish to create.
   - Imagine a calming scene.
   - Follow a guided journey.
   - Sit in contemplation, perhaps while looking at a candle flame.
   - Focus on bodily sensations or on your breath.
   - Simply sit in silence.

   Generally speaking, the purpose of the various methods of meditation is as a vehicle to still your conscious mind and open the doorway to your higher awareness, that is connected to ALL that is. From this place, your higher wisdom can flow towards you.

   As a general rule, the recommended time frame for a meditation is 15 to 20 minutes. Sometimes that will seem to go in a flash, and other times it can feel like forever, particularly if your mind and energy are busy or distracted.

   An additional benefit is that regular meditation practice has been demonstrated to have significant long-term health and wellbeing benefits.

Silence is golden

Practice some simple silence from time to time, where you are not *efforting* or focusing on anything in particular, but rather just *being*. This is incredibly replenishing to your spirit and offers space for some wonderful creative ideas to flow through into your consciousness.

2. **Connecting with nature** is a powerful way to slow down and tune-in to your self. See Chapter 9, 'Your Relationship with Earth and Nature', for further details.

3. **Participate in activities that slow you down and help you relax** e.g. have a sauna, immerse in a bath, receive a massage, do some craft work, take a nap, sit and contemplate nature.

Intuition speaks in many forms.
You can discover your own unique repertoire
if you are open to listening.

6.
The Voice of Your Intuition

Sometimes the voice of intuition is loud, but most often it is a still, quiet voice. This is why having times of slowing down, grounding and centring yourself is extremely helpful to calm the noise of your life in order for you to hear the quiet, often gentle, communication of your intuition.

Intuition also speaks in many forms. You can discover your own unique repertoire if you are open to listening. Methods of receiving guidance are varied for everyone because intuition speaks a range of languages. Your intuition will talk to you in ways you can most easily relate to and recognise.

Languages of intuition

Physical sensations: Your body literally *speaks* to you with a range of physical sensations which can include the following.

Goose bumps – These may arise when someone shares a story that resonates with you or when you relate a meaningful story of your own to others.

Gut feelings – Some people experience strong sensations of butterflies, nausea or pain in their stomach or digestive area as physical guidance.

Twinges or chills – Sensations can vary from chills down your spine to a pang of fear or a twinge that may stop you in your tracks, or perhaps you may experience one that is uniquely yours.

Hunches – When you have a *hunch* about something, it may feel like a knowing or confirming sensation that you are on the right track, even though you may have no explanation for it at the time.

Hearing: The *sound* of your intuition may be delivered in a number of ways.

Words - You may hear words, phrases or sentences spoken by others which *stand out in bold* to you with their meaning.

Music - Maybe you hear songs or parts of songs that seem to have relevance or perhaps provide an answer to a question you have been contemplating.

Messages - Some people *hear* meaningful messages or whole statements in their mind that provide guidance or affirmation. In some instances, these messages appear as words which seem to jump off the page or screen.

Vision: Visual intuition can be some of the most impacting and can arrive in a range of forms.

Visions - Insight can come in the form of receiving a vision in your mind's eye that has meaning for you. These messages can be direct and obvious, or sometimes they are symbolic and metaphoric, where you may need to explore the symbology to understand its special meaning.

Pictures – Simple images, photos and pictures can flash into your mind's eye as a clear message from your intuition. These can appear in full colour or black and white, either singly or in a linked series of meanings. They may also be repetitive and increase in frequency.

Dreams - Dreams can also be a form of vision and are filled with symbolic messages. You can develop the skills to interpret them. There are many books on the subject of dream analysis, so you could choose one using the guidance of your intuition. In the practical steps section at the end of Chapter 9, there is a process called 'Nature's Reflection' - you can utilise this to understand the message of your visions and dream symbols.

Feelings and Emotions: We can have a myriad of emotions in a day, and not all of them are going to be intuitive guidance. However, as described more fully in Chapter 3, emotions can absolutely act as insight and direction in life.

For example, fear can be a message to be careful or perhaps

an indication of new ground to be traversed. Anger or feeling resistance to something could be your intuition saying *no* and to set limits, excitement, even in its finest nuance, can indicate a *move* toward a choice, and experiencing passion for something, feeling *driven*, having a desire or feeling impetus can all be your inner navigation system leading you toward something good in your life.

Love: Love is the glue that can magnetise your intuitive experience into fruition. It can offer powerful guidance for your best choices. You may receive a sense of *knowing in your heart* about the right actions to take. Your heart can also guide you in integrity around a situation or choice. Compassion for a situation or someone can lead you to make a beneficial contribution to their life. In addition, love acts as a potent bond and line of intuitive communication between people. Any feelings of, "I would love to..." can be a sign of direction for you. (See Chapter 4 for further information.)

Knowing: Whole-concept knowing can be another form of intuition. Sometimes people simply *know* things and receive that understanding with a sense of insight. Inspired or creative ideas for action, projects, and solutions also fall into this category.

Signs: Signs are physical things, moments or events that stand out in your world.

Objects - Perhaps a book seemingly falls off the shelf at you, or is given to you, that provides answers to questions you have been contemplating.

Signs - Maybe a road sign you pass or an advertising billboard appears to convey a special message. Seemingly by chance someone appears to speak the solution to a problem you have been thinking about, this too can be a sign.

The Natural World - Nature is full of possible signs that can reflect an answer, reassurance or guidance in some way. For example, seeing a rainbow at a poignant moment, an animal crossing your path which has special or symbolic meaning, or cloud formations designing a picture message that seems exclusively for you.

Intuition has a unique tonality

ALL the communications from your intuition can be interpreted by your feelings. You might ask yourself, "Was that a message?"

Messages will have a certain tonality about them, so that they *feel* like a communication to you, even though your sense of this may be quite subtle. It will resonate within you in a particular manner, or the message will stand out to you in some way because of the special feeling accompanying it. As you build relationships with your intuitive communications, you will learn to recognise their unique tonality.

An awareness of this feeling tone is worth developing because this will ultimately lead to a natural flow between recognising the messages you receive, responding with action, and the subsequent positive outcomes in your life as a result. It may take some time, but with practice you will recognise this unique tonality with increasing awareness until it becomes an almost instant recognition.

Signs include synchronicity

Synchronicity is when certain events show-up in your life which appear to be giving you a sign. Synchronicity can validate many aspects of intuition. For example, that you are on track, you are being guided towards a certain direction or particular choice, as well as indicating the best timing for action. For instance, you may experience this when something you want or are thinking about *magically* shows up in your world, or you are planning to contact a friend and they phone you, or things wonderfully fall into place on a project. With the power of synchronicity, it is as if all your *ducks line up in a row,* so if you are looking for an answer to a question, the solution will simply be provided, or you wish to manifest an item or situation and it appears right in front of you in the course of your day. These are all clear examples of the magic of synchronicity in your life.

Synchronicity usually has some aspect of benevolence within it as things flow or communicate for your higher good, so it delivers some good or a sense of gifting into your life. You may feel as if the Universe has lined up in your favour and there is loving experience involved. There could also be a sense of everyone benefitting from the situation if others are involved.

Deanne - Synchronicity Delivers Flowers

"I was experiencing deep sadness after my dog had disappeared in a storm and had been feeling painful loss. I noticed a repeated yearning to have some flowers in my house. I had even witnessed myself feeling I wished someone would give me some. Out of the blue, and to my surprise, a neighbour and friend phoned to say, "I want to bring you some flowers." She delivered to me an absolutely beautiful bunch of fresh flowers from her garden that brightened my days for a full week. I was so grateful she trusted her intuition to gift me the flowers."

Julie - Travel When Everybody Wins

"I had been contemplating a holiday to visit my mother – I had two options for a time to visit but was undecided. As her health was declining, I didn't want to delay my visit much longer and prayed for the best timing to become clear to me. Around that stage, my father mentioned he would love to go away on a little holiday with my brother and visit some of his old golfing mates. However, he didn't want to leave my mother alone, so I suggested I could visit and take care of her while he went away. My brother worked shift work and I knew from previous conversations, any trip needed to happen within one of his roster breaks. I also only had a ten-day window in which I could travel amongst my other commitments. So, I emailed him to discuss his schedule. As it so happened, his shift break was perfectly timed within my ten-day window.

My timing was clear. I went to stay with Mum for those ten days, which she absolutely loved, and my father had a wonderful holiday break. It was my birthday during this time, so I was able to enjoy a lovely celebration with my mother while on holidays in a stunning seaside environment. This turned out to be the last birthday I would celebrate with Mum. Synchronicity certainly took care of me and guided the perfect timing for all."

These two examples depict beautifully the benevolence within synchronicity and how everyone can benefit.

Benevolent synchronicity

Synchronicity can involve the bringing together of people for a greater good. A divinely planned arrangement that has a healing element or goodness at its centre and perhaps leads you on to greater things. There is also an element of higher purpose in the meeting that may or may not be obvious to begin with, but you come away feeling good about the connection or experience. Ultimately, it has relationship at its centre – it is the interaction of those involved that contains benevolence and may have compassion at its foundation.

It could be as simple as a chance meeting and momentary exchange, or it may have a grander design.

Eva - Synchronicity Affirms Purpose

"After 35 years of work, I retired. Without a job to hang my hat on, I felt unsure of my purpose for about a month. I had been aware many years previous that *kindness* was a high personal value of mine. However, I had always felt my *purpose* had to be bigger and better than that.

During this phase of contemplation, I attended my regular support group and, while discussing values, I mentioned that something I held highly is kindness. In the following week, I completed an online questionnaire on values, and not surprisingly, it showed that kindness was one of my highest values.

Within a few weeks of this, a friend invited me to an interview she was running with two international indigenous poets. I reviewed the event online and felt drawn to attend. An Aboriginal woman and a Native American Indian woman were being interviewed, and the essence of their stories related to dealing with loss and memories. Throughout the interviews, the word *kindness* kept being spoken. The Aboriginal woman mentioned, "I lose myself sometimes and get caught up in things," meaning at times she would lose the sense of connection with her essence, become busy and lose sight of her true values. She reflected on her mother and said, "When she died, she was remembered as a woman of kindness."

This touched my heart incredibly deeply because it had allowed me to see clearly where true values lie. Intuitively, I felt this was a deep affirmation from these spiritually strong, heartfelt women who had a soul connection to the earth. I experienced within me a shift of knowing absolutely in my heart that kindness is my deep purpose, beyond whatever I might do for work."

Penny - Grandmothers Come Full Circle

"The first time I met my neighbour, after 14 years of living close-by, was on a routine dog walk. Anne and I had only ever had the chance to wave from afar occasionally when I was walking my dog. Anne then acquired a dog herself and began walking her dog in my street. One afternoon, I arrived late home from work and took my dog for our usual afternoon stroll to the end of my cul-de-sac, and there we met Anne who was also walking her dog. We started chatting about our lives and she mentioned the name of a regional town where her grandmother had lived and owned a hotel from 1925 to 1965. I recognised it as the hotel where my Nan (my mum's mother) had worked when she was 15 years old, from 1925 to 1933. Further discussion revealed that my Nan had worked for Anne's grandmother, who in turn had treated her like family all those years ago! Anne mentioned that although her grandmother had passed, her aunt was still alive at 99 years of age and was the keeper of the family photos, which likely included photos of my Nan. Naturally, I was astounded and delighted and said I would love to see them if possible.

Two weeks passed and I thought maybe the photos would not surface. Out of the blue, Anne phoned to say her aunt had indeed remembered my Nan and described her perfectly as, "A tiny little thing with frizzy hair." A memory of 85 years ago! Her aunt had found four photos of my Nan and posted them to Anne.

When I collected the photos, I discovered three of them were of Nan's wedding in 1933. My Nan had produced copies of the photos back then and sent them to Anne's grandmother as a gift. Two of these photos my family had never seen - one being a beautiful colour-touched photo of Nan holding and lovingly looking down on her wedding bouquet. A wonderful surprise was that each of the wedding photos had my Nan's handwriting on the back. The fourth picture was a hotel staff group photo taken in 1928, which included my Nan, who was about 18 years old at the time. How wonderful!

During this time, my mother was living in a low-care nursing facility. I arranged for the colour-touched photo to be enlarged and framed. It took pride of place on my mum's dressing table, and she happily told everyone who visited, "That's my mum on her wedding day."

As it turned out, Anne's aunt passed away just three months later. Those photos would have been lost forever had we not bumped into each other at the end of my street. What incredible synchronicity to retrieve those treasured family photos and in perfect timing to bless my mother with a gorgeous and previously unseen picture of her mum and for me to reconnect with happy memories of my Nan."

Maggie - Old Friends Reunited with Higher Purpose

"A girlfriend and I began our friendship during our teenage years, in the mid-1970s which swirled with music, bands, boys, sex, drugs and rock 'n' roll. My friend fell pregnant at 15 years old and had a baby son. Soon afterwards, she became pregnant again. However, this time, her baby was adopted from birth. When I finished school, we all shared a house in the city together, along with another friend, splitting the rent, working and partying.

After a couple of years, I travelled overseas and our lives led us in different directions, reconnecting briefly as young mothers before our lives once again progressed along separate paths.

Thirty-five years later - to present time - I was in the situation of raising my granddaughter, as my daughter was dealing with drug addiction. My old friend had been on my mind, and I was wondering if she had ever been in touch with her adopted child. Around that same time, I attended the local Blues Festival to see Patti Smith perform, which in turn triggered further memories of those early years together and deepened my longing to reconnect.

I attempted to find her via Google searches but had no luck. I happened to share my wonderings, longings and festival stories with a close friend over the phone. The very next week, she met up with another mutual friend in a clothing store, and through their conversation, they were able to locate my old friend. Amazing! I learned that she had in fact been searching for me also.

We reconnected over the phone, through tears of joy we discovered our life stories were running in tandem. Her first son had also become victim to drug addiction and as a result she was also caring for her granddaughter. I was delighted to discover that indeed her second child, who had been adopted, recently found her and they were beginning their relationship.

It has been very emotional and uplifting to be back in touch. We've been able to be of great support to each other once again, sharing similar life experiences as grandmother carers."

These stories are wonderful examples of how benevolent synchronicity can bring people together for the greater good of all, in this case, affirming true purpose and reuniting families and friends.

Intuition has innate timing

Intuitive messages have within them an innate timing. This timing will often be beyond your capacity to predict or your logical understanding. It will be as if there is a hand guiding the perfect unfolding of your life. Often, in retrospect, you will see that following your intuition was linked to an incredible and beautiful wisdom of when to act. Your logical mind, which operates within a limited view, may not be able to see the possible outcomes of the messages you receive, and go *crazy* with doubts and questions about following your intuitive messages. With practise and trust, you can teach your logical mind to sit in the back seat a little and accept that you have another aspect of your consciousness that *knows* divine right timing and can be relied upon.

As you learn to trust the flow of your intuition, there can be a wonderful unfolding in your life, seemingly like magic. You will see that your intuition speaks to you throughout the day in many ways, and this can create an ease that saves you time and energy that is beyond your ability to design.

Our intuition is always attempting to create ease and flow.

Gill - Gift Giving Made Easy

"I was looking for a pair of slippers for a friend's birthday gift. I had researched online and found the perfect pair on sale; however, an online purchase would not arrive in time. The department store where the slippers were on sale was 40 minutes' drive away, and I didn't have the time to drive there during my work week. On her birthday, I waited until I felt good timing to phone to wish her happy birthday. When she answered the phone, I discovered she was in the shopping centre walking toward the very department store where the slippers were located. Perfect timing! She was able to pick them up for herself on her birthday."

Tania - Saving Time

"For the last year or so, I've become increasingly aware of my intuition and try to follow it. However, there are times when I am in a hurry and fail to listen to the messages. For example, I will be packing my bag for work and notice a thought rush through my mind that I haven't seen my work keys. I'll halt that little voice with an inner comment such as, "Of course they are in the bottom of my bag," but not actually check. Then, I arrive at work and discover the keys are actually missing from my bag, necessitating a drive home to get them! I find this happens to me when I'm in a rush and don't take time to properly listen to my intuition – it certainly would save me time if I listened."

Cheryl - Intuition Indicates Priorities

"A pile of 'non-priority' mail had accumulated on my desk, and I kept thinking I should sort it out. My washing machine broke down unexpectedly, and with the machine full of washing and baskets piling up rapidly from my three children, I made an unscheduled trip to the store to buy a new machine. When I pulled out my wallet to use my interest-free store card, I discovered it was out of date with the new one sitting on my desk at home in that pile of 'non-priority' mail. If I had just listened to that *little voice*, it would have saved me an hour of precious time at the store sorting that out."

Intuition can guide us to perfect timing for our situation.

Emily - Parenting and Timing

"I use my intuition when parenting my teenage son. Sometimes he becomes worked-up about something, and even though I know we need to talk, I intuitively feel it is not the right time to bring the issue up with him. Once, he was angry with me for days. Finally, one morning, after attempting to comfort him and being rejected, I left his room only to experience, about an hour later, a strong feeling that the time had come to talk. I was sitting downstairs and had an overwhelming feeling that he needed me. I went straight to him, and he let go, and we just hugged. I could feel the release of tension and was grateful I was aware of my intuition and had followed it immediately."

Irene - A Holiday Comes Together

"I have been a gypsy wanderer all my life and have found when I embark on a journey, whether it's a long one or a short day trip, my intuition takes over strongly. The energy begins with a feeling of excitement and freedom. I feel very balanced and a powerful sense of trust kicks in. I always begin by calling in the *Light* to guide and protect me first, and off I go into an unknown adventure.

For example, my husband and I were invited to a 60th birthday party at my friend's property interstate. I wanted to fly in early and catch up with some girlfriends first. A week before we were due to leave, I started to feel uneasy about my husband going with me. I noticed what I really desired was to visit my girlfriends in the city on my own and then have him join us for the birthday celebrations afterward – I knew he wouldn't enjoy the first leg of the trip anyway.

The night before we were due to fly, he had a dental emergency, which required attention the next morning. Our dilemma was whether he should still go on the trip at all as he was in acute pain. At the same time, I felt strongly he should be there at the 60th celebrations. After some discussion, we decided to cancel his flight, which was refunded by the airline. My husband had his tooth fixed, and amazingly, his best friend, who resides in another state, was in town and driving down to the party, so was able to give my husband a ride all the way there.

I began the first leg of the journey on my own and had a lovely time connecting with all my girlfriends, and then a fun and pleasurable drive to the property. This was followed by a wonderful time camping with 20 other people, including my husband, for our friend's 60th birthday celebrations.

Throughout this process, my intuition had been speaking to me and synchronicity had fallen into place, though somewhat unexpectedly. With perfect timing, everyone was taken care of and we both experienced a really enjoyable journey and celebration."

Not what I wanted to hear

Sometimes your intuition is going to tell you things you don't want to hear or take action upon, while at the same time the message will have a sense of *being the right choice*.

Amy - Difficult Decisions

"At times, I ponder what seem to be difficult decisions in my life and ask for the right action to move through me. I might wake at night or in the morning just knowing what I need to do. Even though I know what action to take, sometimes it can be very difficult to follow through with my decision. It might take a few days until I work up the nerve to take action, but I know what has to be done and step through it.

At one stage, I was having challenges in a long-term relationship. We had been working through several issues for quite some time and had been receiving counselling. I am someone who will work on things rather than give up easily, especially in relationships where things do take time and effort. At the same time, I was contemplating the right direction. Eventually, I simply woke up one morning and *knew in my heart* that the relationship was over. Part of me didn't really want to hear that, but I knew it was the truth, so immediately acted to gently and decisively complete that relationship. I felt deep sadness and it was not easy, but knew it was the best action for myself."

Sarah - A Serious Health Issue Needing Attention

"I was three months away from my annual breast scan, having had two previous breast cancers, when I had a strong feeling to have my scan early. Often, I would ignore these feelings, telling myself I was being paranoid. While this intuition was not welcome or a comfortable feeling, I trusted it on this occasion. I am glad I did as the scan detected another cancer and when the doctors removed the tumour, they found a second tiny one in the same breast. Early detection is so important."

Jane - Please Don't Leave

"I was living in an amenable house share arrangement with a young fellow. He was renting my spare room, which was providing extra income for me. The arrangement was working and flowing well, and I wanted him to stay on for a while. The meld in a shared household is so important for a happy living situation. I was aware of some instability in his life situation but was hoping this would settle. I then had a dream where he told me he was moving on, and when I awoke, I tried to ignore this. A month later, I had another dream in which he told me he was leaving, and I still was hoping I wasn't right.

The next week, he told me he was moving out. Even though I wasn't surprised, as my dreams had pre-warned me, I definitely did not want to hear this. In the end, it all worked out perfectly. A month later, an even better share situation evolved for me – one that was way more settled, which was ultimately what I desired. This whole scenario highlighted to me that my fear of loss can get in the way of trusting my intuition and also in trusting that something even better might be on its way. It pays to trust."

Listening is the key

It is up to you to embrace your unique lines of intuitive communication. You can achieve this by listening to the still quiet messages being given to you. Don't let them go by. Respond to your intuition like a beloved friend. In this way, you build a more intimate relationship with your Higher Knowing.

A great analogy for this is in a form of bodywork called Body Harmony, which is based on listening to the flow of energy in the body. It involves placing the hands on the body and sensitively *listening* to the natural flow of energy that exists there, supporting it and allowing it to unwind without imposing any agenda; it's simply about receiving the flow that exists within the body.

A similar process is at play with your intuition. The first step is to pay attention and then to *listen* to what's there and allow the flow.

Allowing

Receiving your intuition all the way through, from recognising your guidance to taking some action, is a process of allowing without judgment. You may find that at times you still judge or question your knowing, but over time the tonality will become so familiar that you'll learn to put doubts aside, choosing to allow and follow it instead. This allowing takes practice until you have built familiarity with your intuition, but it is empowering to reach this stage.

You know you are allowing when you experience the receiving of what you want. This can be in the form of information you're seeking, or a sense of creative flow, perhaps a material possession, or even when you receive a quality of life experience you're desiring, such as joy or love or personal satisfaction. Synchronicity is also a sign that you are allowing, as in this instance, you are receiving the flow of life.

Next are some practical activities to embrace the *allowing* of your intuitive flow.

Practical Steps to Opening the Channels of Intuitive Communication

Responding to the messages

Acknowledging and being grateful for the messages in your life, and then acting on them in some way, is the best method to open the channels and establish clearer communication with the unique repertoire of your intuition.

1. **Acknowledge:** If you receive a physical sensation, such as goose bumps or a gut feeling, you can say in acknowledgement, "Wow! I've got goose bumps when you tell me that," or you might say, "I have a gut feeling about this."

    If you receive a message, say, "Thanks!" In this way, you are saying, "Yes, I heard you," and are acknowledging the message.

2. **Take some action on the message:** If you have been asking for answers on a subject or looking for direction in an aspect of life and you receive a sign, take some action to back yourself up.

3. **You can invoke synchronicity in your life:**

    You can ask for synchronicity to show up in your life and ask to be aware of it when it does.

    Simply speak your intent out loud with purpose:

    Generic examples:

    "I welcome benevolent synchronicity in my life. I intend for the presence-of-being to recognise it and the courage to take beneficial action."

    "I am allowing synchronous events to guide my life."

Specific examples on certain subjects:

*"I ask for synchronicity ...... (on whatever subject you wish) ......
to guide my way."*

*"Let the synchronicities come together to guide my choices
in regard to......"*

*"I am now in the flow of receiving the most beneficial
outcome in regard to......"*

*"I am in the pathway of those people whom I will most
benefit from meeting, and they me."*

*Wonderful outcomes can unfold as a result
of surrendering to the power of the unknown
and allowing yourself to be guided
by intuition and synchronicity.*

7.

What Do You Want?

Having clarity about what you want is an important first step in allowing yourself to receive it. You can then allow your intuition to guide you to the most beneficial action toward your desired outcome. This means simply following your inner guidance throughout the course of your day.

It does not mean actively pursuing your intuition to guide you, but rather identifying something you want and then letting go. It can be within the most unexpected moments that what you want will *magically* show up in your life. Often it will be synchronicity that guides you, or your heart felt desires can show-up through following your motivations along the way.

Use your intuition to guide you

Once you are clear about what you want, you can use your intuition to guide you there.

Kathy - Crystals Manifest

"I had been in the process of redecorating my home and feeling I wanted more healing crystals to display around the interior. My small collection of crystals included a gorgeous large amethyst crystal cave, which I had received as a 50th birthday gift.

One of the ways I like to shop is to explore second-hand stores for clothes and other bits and pieces. My work requires me to drive extensively around my local area. On a typical workday, not long after my crystal idea, I was inspired to drop into a second-hand store as I was driving past. I entered the store to find a wonderful array of crystals that someone had dropped in the very day prior! I had never seen this in a second-hand shop before.

There was a brilliant red quartz ball measuring fifteen centimetres, several pieces of citrine and rose quartz, and some smaller crystals. I purchased the entire collection at an incredibly discounted price and continue to love and enjoy them displayed around my home!"

Megan - Clothes Shopping Handled

"I was gifted a pair of bright candy-striped trousers, which I absolutely loved, and had been searching everywhere for a blouse to go with them. Shopping for something that matched had turned into an effort, so I decided to stop looking.

A couple of weeks later, I needed to visit my bank and was concerned about parking availability in the lunchtime rush-hour. While driving there, I had a sudden impulse to travel a different route than usual and found an easy park around the corner from the bank. I then noticed my parking spot was directly outside a recycled clothing store and experienced an instant feeling to go in and have a look. There I found the perfect blouse to go with those trousers and used it for years with many outfits."

Kim - Using Intuition for Self-Care

"I desired to lose some weight but knew I needed support and direction as my previous efforts had been unsuccessful. I didn't initiate action straight away as I felt overwhelmed by the many weight loss programs available. One day, I was walking through a local street market, and there happened to be a stall promoting weight loss. I noticed that I felt motivated to talk to the people at the stand. I researched the product and decided it made sense and also felt right to me. As a result, I successfully reduced two dress sizes over three months."

In each of these examples, the desire was identified and then, by simply following intuitive guidance in the course of life without agenda, the perfect outcomes unfolded.

Confirming your desire

When you have an inspired idea but are unsure if it is what you want, you may feel the need to clarify. Pushing on doors was discussed in a previous chapter as a way of exploration of an idea, however, the *door to explore* may need to be identified within the course of your life, or you could ask for further guidance.

Karen – To Grey or Not to Grey

"I was approaching 60 years of age and had been considering the idea to stop having my hair regularly coloured and fully receive my grey hair look. I was tired of the hair colouring round-about. In addition, I was exclusively using organic hair dyes to minimise the chemical impact on my body, but even those were making me feel unwell, and I began to dread going to the hairdresser.

For a couple of years, I had been toying with the idea, but felt more comfortable covering up my grey hair, and staying with what I believed to be a more youthful look. On occasion during those years, I discussed the idea with a close friend. One day, seemingly out of the blue, she messaged me a link to a Facebook Group for women only, called Going Grey Gracefully. I joined the group and found it to be rich with incredibly kind and positive women supporting each other in stepping through the process of growing out their grey hair. With around 150,000 members, it was obvious there were a large number of women seeking loving input through the process.

After connecting with the group for a while, I felt buoyed and inspired by women sharing their stories, and my decision became clear. I wanted to go ahead with my transformation and never looked back. I not only grew out my grey, I had my long hair cut short, and now look completely different in this phase of my life. I love my grey hair appearance and it has provided me a sense of freedom I had not anticipated. I enjoy relaxing into this more authentic expression of me and celebrate easy-to-manage hair, having more money available to spend on myself, and no more chemical dyes to contend with."

In this story, we see the impetus to make a personal change, transformed into clarity of what she wanted via the process of a Facebook group suggestion from a friend, which guided and backed her way forward. The Universe is benevolent and will offer support to your desire to help you gain clarity. Be open to following the flow and synchronicities related to your desire.

Joanne – Asking for Clarity

"I grew up on a farm in a regional area with fruit trees and chickens and loved it. As an adult, for many years, my home was within a beautiful bushland setting at the outer edge of a large city. For a long time, I played with the idea of moving right away from the city to a regional area. I yearned for a sense of increased space and an even more peaceful existence. I was never really sure if this was doable, nor clearly assessed the plus or minus considerations, and in addition, I was unclear if my partner would ever be keen to leave our already happy existence.

One of my regular early morning pleasures was to walk through local bushland, where I would gain a sense of centre and balance for the start of my workdays. Connecting with nature has always brought a sense of calm and clarity to me. I was participating in Diana's Intuitive Mastery Program and at one meeting we discussed the concept of asking for guidance. The very next morning, I decided to consciously call on guidance around my desire to move to the country. As I walked along my usual track, I came across several white feathers on the path. I had never seen this before, and I felt immediately that they were a sign. I *knew* the feathers were significant and I experienced insight that morning we were on the right path to pursue moving.

The clarity of what I wanted had moved from my head to my heart, and I knew in every fibre of my being that my desire was on track. Our home was assessed for valuation and the figures revealed there would be enough funds to purchase in the regional area we dreamed of, as well as free up some finances for future living. On discussion, my partner was fully on board with the idea, and we started pushing on doors by researching real estate in our desired location. Everything flowed to support our move. We found a property we were keen to view – four acres of land with a large lake, established gardens, fruit trees, a hen house and stunning country surrounds. Because of Covid border restrictions at the time, we were not able to fly interstate to view the property. However, a friend who lived nearby was able to walk through with the real estate agent, beaming us in via FaceTime to see the house and land. We loved everything about the place. We were successful with our bidding to buy the property, and subsequently sold our home, all within a three-week period. The doors flung open, providing further affirmation we were on track. It was all systems go for our move to the country."

This story offers the example of asking for clarity about what you want when you are unsure about your desire. In this case, her request for guidance brought the concept of moving from an attractive idea to a full-body, heartfelt knowing of what she wanted. Once you know the truth in the cells of your body your guidance will be clear. The other reflection in the story is the magnetic power of her heart's desire, drawing synchronicities and flow into manifestation for the creation of her desired move. In addition, confirmation of direction was provided by multiple synchronicities and the ease that occurred as she took action.

What do you want?

This seems like a simple question. However, sometimes we can have difficulty defining exactly what we want in our lives. Many people find themselves feeling, "I don't know what I want." In this instance, you can go back to basics and simply *intend for clarity* on what you want. Then gently be open and *listen out* for intuitive signals, synchronicity and guidance in the process of your life that is moving you toward the deeper knowing of what you *do want*. Wonderful outcomes can unfold as a result of surrendering to the power of the unknown and allowing yourself to be guided by intuition and synchronicity. Your role is to take action on those signs as they cross your path, gradually forging your way forward in safe steps. Things may become clear reasonably quickly or can take a long period of time to gradually unfold.

In the following story, you will see how this woman lands in an uncertain future regarding her career. She kept letting go into the unknown, following the signs along the way over an extended period of time, until she became clear on what made her heart sing for her future.

Robin - Career and Finances Unfolding

"I was working as an Acting Teaching Principal in a regional area. In order to achieve my financial goals, I had moved to a regional position to both advance my career and increase my income. I was also hoping to improve my work-life balance. Financially, I wanted to increase my investments and also needed to fund my son's university education. Despite the challenges of living remotely, away from family and friends, the teaching principal role had provided the opportunity for many satisfying achievements. So, after 18 months, I made the decision, I would continue with the job long-term.

Very suddenly, the previous principal decided to return, and the rug was pulled on my position. I was shocked and immediately faced with a number of questions - what next? How do I maintain my financial position? What do I really want to do now in my career?

I achieved the financial and work goals I set for the past two years, and this had given me confidence I could achieve my goals for the next two years. Reflecting on my previous game plan helped me realise my desire for work-life balance had not panned out at all. In fact, my workload as a school principal for the previous two years had been extreme. I was feeling burnt-out, unhappy and lonely, so decided to rest over the holiday period and take time to consider what I really wanted. I knew I had no energy for packing up the house in the holidays and decided to trust my desire to remain where I was for the time being.

What followed was a complete rest. During this time, several relief positions as acting principals became available in my regional area. These were in very low-stress environments for the subsequent school term, so gave me space to be at ease and further consider what I really wanted. They were also a chance to work in different school situations and help me gain more certainty on future choices.

Intuitively, I knew to withhold from pushing on any doors but rather to sit back and wait for clarity. I had a sense right from the beginning that I was following my intuition. I felt it wasn't the best choice to leave the regional area in which I'd settled but was unable to see how my life was going to pan out. My previous behaviour would have been to decide what I wanted and push on all the doors to get it done. But I couldn't decide what I wanted and just knew to let it unfold.

One of my key loves in teaching, and where I believed I could make a significant contribution, was in behaviour co-ordinating, assisting children to find more balance and focus at school. This aspect of teaching increasingly felt a career direction I wanted to pursue. However, those roles were generally advertised outside my regional area, and even though I attempted to apply for positions, I didn't get a look-in. I kept feeling there was something I still didn't know – something saying to me, "Just wait."

Another driving desire I experienced was to live at a rural coastal area where I had previously resided much earlier in my life. I moved away to make it easier for my son to visit his father and to be closer to the support of my parents. Now I had good friends living there and I wanted to go back and be with my *tribe*. However, I did not have any view of how I could live there and fulfil my financial goals at the same time. It was a very popular location and difficult to get a transfer there as a principal or even deputy principal.

I continued to accept relieving principal positions in my regional area for two more school terms, still wondering what I was going to do with my career. I was offered a relief position at a small school, and I knew I could have that job permanently if I wanted it. On contemplating that idea, it was then I realised I no longer wanted to live remotely. Intuitively, I knew it wasn't right.

I decided to attempt a move to the coast and sent out 40 emails of enquiry. As a result, I was offered a teaching position, and even though this would result in a substantial pay cut, I wanted to do it. I placed all my things in storage, made the move, and took up the job. However, by the end of the first term, I came to the realisation I didn't want to be a teacher in the classroom anymore. I was altogether burned out.

During this unsettled period, my brother and family came to visit. He related how his daughter was receiving tutoring and how much she loved it. He described how it had changed her attitude to school and helped her rekindle a love of learning. Then he said, "You should do this. You'd be really good at it."

On hearing these words, I immediately knew this was right for me. I had a sense of feeling complete, calm and centred. I knew I was going to do it. I had sat uncomfortably in the unknown for a long time, hadn't tried to figure it out, and now my direction was clear.

I immediately pulled out my phone and looked into the tutoring business online. I made enquiries and did my due diligence. During this three-month process, things felt right to me – there was no question.

I did wonder how I was going to finance this new venture. However, a range of financial support came to the fore with relative ease. Three months later, I negotiated my franchise agreement and signed a lease. Six months later, I opened the doors of my new tutoring business.

I now feel at a turning point in my life, still a little in the unknown as I am on a huge learning curve, but solidly on track. All the things I wanted for my future are within the realms of my business – a fulfilling career that utilises my skills to help children thrive at school; the same level of income as a principal or more; being my own boss; and free time during the school holidays.

My future feels bright, with the opportunity to eventually leverage myself out of the business into a manager role, providing even more time and lifestyle freedom."

For this woman, gaining true clarity of what she wanted was an evolution of events, insights and motivations over many months. It included long periods of time simply *being* and *trusting in the process*. This is a perfect example of how sometimes there will be an unfolding of experiences, meetings, and timing that needs to occur before your pathway becomes clear. Your intuition might be motivating you toward something that is out of your purview or leading you toward an even greater outcome than you could conceive for yourself. Your Higher Self knows what potentials are ahead and can lead you to the most beneficial unfolding, especially when you have built a relationship of trust with your intuition.

As a postscript to this story, this woman's business has progressed from strength-to-strength, full of reward and purpose, with children thriving under her tutoring program. As the business has expanded, she has been able to leverage herself by employing a business manager. It certainly served her to keep letting go into the unknown, following her intuition and synchronicities along the way, until the clarity of what she wanted unfolded.

The goal post moved

Sometimes we think we know what we want, and then, in the pursuit of our goal, we discover we actually want something else – that's life. It is wise to stay open to receiving even greater outcomes when working toward something in your life. Stepping forward while remaining open to signs or any resistance along the way can lead you to an even better result.

Alice - Best Outcomes Revealed

"My partner and I had been renting a beautiful rural property on acreage and were happily settled after several years of living there. We had ultimate peace and privacy, beautiful countryside views, a separate cottage on the land for guests, and a deck with an outdoor spa overlooking the scenery. We loved it and wanted to stay there. We felt devastated when the owners decided to sell. After some discussion, we decided to apply for a home loan and make a bid on the house. Unfortunately, the maximum loan available to us was lower than the asking price.

Although I had my heart set on living there permanently, our bid was rejected and I felt devastated again. However, this whole process led us to start looking at other properties to purchase rather than rent. After searching online for houses, we discovered 45 acres of forested land, which had been tenderly cared for by the owners, fronted an enormous picturesque dam and had a renovated shed on it for living. One of our family members joined our discussions and decided to invest with us, so we had sufficient funds to achieve the required loan.

We moved in six weeks later and absolutely love our home. It has turned out to be the perfect place – a safer layout for our young children as well as our two dogs, two cats and ten chooks! We have wonderful forest walks, water views from our house site, a lovely street community, and we are now closer to town with much easier access to everything we need, including schools and the commute to work."

This was definitely a much better outcome for this family than they originally envisioned, achieved through pushing on doors, going with the flow, and following the signs along the way.

Practical Steps for Clarifying
What You Want

Knowing what you want is the perfect place to start for powerful creation in your life. Your intuition and synchronicities can then guide you towards the outcome you desire.

What do I want?

Ask yourself this question, "What do I truly want?"[16]

When you find you are not happy or comfortable with a situation:

1. **Ask yourself – "OK, what do I want?"** Consider what might be the opposite of your situation. Or ask yourself, "What would I prefer to happen in this situation?"

   In asking these questions, you change the trajectory of your thoughts and focus your creative forces into unfolding something better in your life.

2. **Once you are clear on what you want**, then ask for intuitive guidance to move through you or become obvious to you, regarding the best action to take toward your desired outcome (refer to notes on Intention in Chapter 2).

3. **Then release the situation** for the unfolding of events in your life that are in your highest good. This means not being attached to a particular result or how it may occur, but rather allowing the unfolding. Then following your intuitive guidance as it shows up along the way, trusting this will lead you to the best outcome. This involves trusting that the benevolent flow of the Universe is on your side - more on this in the next chapter.

4. **Take action on your guidance**, *push on doors*. Remember, small-safe-steps.

Mind, body and emotional patterns
may cloud your ability to accurately interpret
and respond to your intuition.

8.

Intuition versus Fantasy

Your personal, family and life history will be perhaps one of the biggest influences on your intuitive clarity. As you explore the expansion of your intuitive ability, you may discover you have patterns of behaviour and beliefs that get in the way of hearing, trusting and following your intuition.

To gain true mastery of your intuitive self, it will be necessary - with patience, self-love and wisdom - to gain awareness and work through any life patterns and beliefs that may restrict your knowing. There are practical suggestions on how you may do this at the end of this chapter.

Mind body and emotional patterns

You have a physical body, and you also have an energy body. Your energy body is sometimes referred to as your aura. Your energy body extends beyond and interfaces with your physical body and contains the patterning of your life and beliefs.

It is generally understood that, based on what happened to you at birth, during childhood, in your family, at school, as well as in your relationships, you will have made decisions about life that influence you throughout your adulthood. These life experiences establish incredibly complex mind, body, and emotional patterns that are interwoven within your energy system. These include both your positive, life-enhancing patterns as well as your limiting beliefs and perceptions. If you believe in previous life experiences, it may be helpful to know that the patterning of those lives are also held within your energy body and can influence your current life.

Mind, body, and emotional patterns affect behaviour and the way you may respond to situations. It is good to keep in mind that there are an abundance of life decisions you have made and life patterns you have established that serve your life and others and are the basis of your unique skills and talents. However, some life patterns and perceptions can cloud the ability to accurately interpret and respond to your intuition. Often, these patterns will be significantly more deeply rooted than you realise.

This is a vast subject, and there are many books written on life patterns and the bias of belief. In this guide, the discussion is limited to the effects on your intuition.

Examples of personal beliefs and life patterns that may affect intuition:

- You may not trust your own knowing because your ideas or abilities were undermined as you were growing up. Perhaps in childhood, an adult told you that you were stupid or that you'd never amount to anything. Perhaps somehow, you received a message that you were not smart enough, or maybe not as clever as your siblings, or perhaps you were shamed by your peers in teenage years. As a result, you do not trust your own knowing.

- As a child, you may have learned, through experience and observation, that being a perfectionist and exhibiting high-performing behaviour will be rewarded with love and praise from your parents. In adulthood, you may continue to aim for an external standard of perfection rather than be in the flow of your own ideas and timing. This may lead to a sense of confusion about what you truly want and even a disconnection from your true passion.

- Perhaps as a teenager you weren't allowed to express sadness, or anger, and as a result, are now disengaged from your emotions. Consequently, you may find it difficult to get in touch with feelings and emotions, which could be providing a valuable guiding force in your life.

- As a young person, were your dreams and visions dismissed by family or peer opinions? If so, this may have caused you to not develop the ability to trust in your dreams and inspirations or believe in your personal ability to achieve them.

· Maybe as a child, you were not allowed to make your own choices as you explored life. In this case, you may have missed the natural learning, confidence and building of a deep sense of self, which occurs through trial and error. As a consequence, you may have difficulty with discernment and making decisions, or backing your knowing, as an adult.

Mind-body-emotional patterns are often operating subconsciously or perhaps semi-consciously, suppressed by emotional denial, so that you may be barely aware of them. The denial happens because the original experience was emotionally painful. As a result of an upset in childhood, you may have suppressed the unpleasant feelings in order to cope, and in so doing, you anchor that pattern in your energy system.

These patterns of experience tend to annoyingly repeat until you identify them and consciously choose to shift them by changing your thoughts, beliefs and emotional response. Sometimes, you may need assistance and guidance to gain insight and understanding as to the patterns you are holding. This is natural and everyone can benefit from support in their healing.

The good news is that views about life and relationships can, and do, change. The speediest and most obvious of these shifts occurs when you have an impactful life experience, such as a serious health diagnosis, a major shock, or a huge loss of some kind. It is as though the very foundation or life is knocked from beneath you and the way you view the world changes very quickly. If you have experienced any big life upheavals, you may have noticed your values change rapidly, or you become very aware of what matters most to you.

Most often, however, changes in perception and beliefs occur step-by-step. The first step is to become aware of them. Being aware of your inner life and how experiences from your past could be influencing your perception and decisions can help you tune in to the messages from your intuition. This then allows you to interpret them and make choices in a more balanced and open manner.

Intuition can be clouded

These mind-body-emotion patterns can, and will, cause blocks or *cloudiness* in the clarity of your intuition. They can also cause confusion between wishing or fearing something to be true (a fantasy) as opposed to accurate intuitive insight.

Amber - Run by My Fear of Loss

"I am a very intuitive person and often accurate. Sometimes, however, I find myself influenced by my past.

A close friend of mine who has a serious health condition has often felt pressured by me when I assume she needs my help. I have perceived a need, but not checked-in with her before stepping-in and attempting to help. She has told me on several occasions that I am being influenced by my fear of loss of her rather than her need for help.

By way of understanding, my father passed away when I was very young, leaving only my mum. A child in this situation can feel vulnerable to the wellbeing of the remaining parent. Now, when I see my friend under stress, a deep part of me is triggered and panics. I rush in to take care of her without asking. My action is being driven by my unconscious need to care for her so that I feel safe, and not by my intuition about her desire for assistance."

As in this example above, the patterning from past trauma can be quite deep-seated, causing our motivations to be influenced by our past.

Jessica - Free the Cat

"I've had a habit in my life of being overly responsible. This tends to result in me taking on more responsibility than required and sometimes jumping ahead with action that is unneeded or unproductive.

This pattern was particularly clear to me when making end-of-life decisions for my ageing cat. He was 18 years old – bless him. I was aware he had limited years ahead and very mindful of not dragging him through a long health demise unnecessarily (how responsible of me!). He had been showing some signs of aging, and I kept feeling maybe it was his time. I phoned my vet and she suggested I make an appointment for a check-up. In the end, despite his advanced age, all his blood work was within normal range and my vet felt he was doing quite well all things considered. She was actually somewhat amused, as she had been expecting a cat to arrive on its last legs! I came home from the appointment realising I was being driven by my pattern of over-responsibility, not my calm intuition. I was overly concerned way ahead of time with due care in his ageing process. My cat lived on happily for another year and I simply knew in my heart when it was time to send him to heaven."

As demonstrated in these stories, by backing up your ideas with some practical steps (a vet visit in one story and simply asking if someone wants help in the other), you can check on the reality of your feelings and intuition.

The influence of attachment

Interpretation of messages can be particularly clouded when there is a strong desire or emotional attachment to an outcome you want. This could apply in any area of your life and is unique to each individual. The attachment to a certain outcome tends to be accentuated in aspects of life that carry a strong emotional charge, such as money, relationships, health or work.

When it seems difficult to discern the difference between your *wishing* and intuition, it can be a matter of testing the waters.

A great example of this is at the beginning of a new relationship, where there can be intense emotions. It can be difficult to discern between intuition and fantasy. The only thing to do is to take things step-by-step.

Natalie - The Intensity of Dating

"I had decided it was time to start dating again. There had been a long gap between relationships for me. Though I had previously resisted the idea, I registered on an internet dating site as I felt it had become a legitimate and accepted way of meeting people (being older, internet dating was a new exploration for me).

Through this online search, I met a man who appeared to have enough in common to meet up for coffee (*safe step*). At that meeting, we had a good connection, and we decided to have a second date. However, I did feel some reservations, particularly about his communication style and what appeared to be quite a dark sense of humour. As we progressed step-by-step through the dating cycle, I experienced feelings of incredible connection, of being in flow, and even a deep love for this man. I really wanted things to work out. At the same time, I couldn't ignore some genuine concerns about certain aspects of his behaviour and communication style.

While there were some real positives in this relationship, in the end, the communication issues escalated, and I decided to finish the relationship after three months. This led me to experience a very deep grieving and letting go – I can only assume this was clearing the way for a better relationship to come."

This is a great example of following intuition and guidance, all the way using safe steps and being aware of the possibility of fantasy, pushing on doors and trusting the process until you become clear on what you want.

The other area of life where confusion between wishing and intuition can be strong, is in relation to money.

Kimberley - Investment Gone Bad

"I had been offered an investment in cryptocurrency, and the business model appeared lucrative and exciting. I did have doubts, particularly regarding the way the business was offered to me with a vision of very profitable outcomes. However, many of my friends were jumping on-board, and I started to fear missing the boat. I am educated in financial matters and aware that the *herd mentality* is never the best time to invest. Usually, by the time everyone is jumping on-board, the best money has been made. Nonetheless, I went ahead with the investment. Two months later, the whole thing crashed, and I lost a $1,000 investment. Luckily, I hadn't invested more funds, and upon reflection, part of me knew there may be something afoot that would bring this investment unstuck."

When making decisions, you can reference your education as part of the process. It can be helpful to combine some logical research together with your intuition as part of your decision-making. Remember, as discussed in Chapter 1, logic can complement your intuition.

Of course, another aspect of misreading our emotions, is when fear and anxiety can get in the way of stepping into more excitement, and this was covered in Chapter 3 on 'Emotions.'

You can't get it wrong

If you discover that you have gone down the track of chasing a fantasy outcome, then this will give you a deeper reference point (knowing from your experience) of your intuition. How does that work? When you are innocently seeking to make good choices, ones that enrich your life and your happiness, then you are making decisions based on what you feel is right. This is the right choice for you at this time. You can NOT get it wrong.

Your experience will soon show you, in retrospect, if you made the best choice and, you will have learned whether you were motivated by fantasy or by your intuition. Sometimes these can be hard lessons in life, and sometimes they are just minor corrections. This gives you clarity for future situations when fantasy is driving you and also improves your recognition of when intuition is speaking to you. In any case, you have had a valuable life experience along the way that can be positively applied to your choices in the future.

Learning comes best through experience – same applies to your intuitive knowing.

The hand of benevolence

There is an incredible hand of benevolence upon the outworking of things in your life. It is as if there is a loving force at play, forever designing the greater good in your life. If you make a choice that you wish to correct, there is usually an answer provided. Things generally seem to have a way of working themselves out in time and often for the better. This is part of the benevolent design of the Universe around you. Have you noticed it?

As mentioned earlier, there are unlimited possibilities in the unfolding of your life. When you are committed to following your unique path, which is in alignment with your highest good, then all will be well. A helpful metaphor is the story of a rocket ship's pathway to the moon. It is rarely directly on track. It is actually regularly off-course, but continuously correcting as it travels. It's okay to go off-course; just make corrections as you go.

Here is one great example of listening to motivations, watching guidance along the way, and making adjustments according to that guidance.

Christine - My Intuition Leads Me Home

"My house is one of three homes on a block of land – a three-plex if you like, but the homes are separated, and each has their own yard. One of the homeowners and I had been experiencing problems with the third homeowner, who wasn't pulling her weight with maintenance of common property and was in significant arrears with her body corporate fees. Despite many discussions about property care over several years, and special arrangements being made for regular payments, there was continued dissonance and her fees remained in abeyance. This situation unsettled me. I was fed up and considering my options.

At the same time, I had been asking myself, "How can I be free of my mortgage?" I love exploring new horizons and often take-off on new explorations when I need a change or feel bogged down, or when I am avoiding something I need to deal with or resolve.

Later that week, I visited a friend, and she suggested I look at homes for sale within her retirement village. She contacted the real estate agent who helped secure her home, and a week later, he showed me a house that fronted a beautiful lake on the village grounds. It had been available for six months as part of a deceased estate and was in the hands of the Public Trustee. Residents needed cash to buy into the village (no loan situations allowed). My calculations indicated that if I sold my home, I would have the cash to buy a house at the village and be free of my mortgage.

I became very excited and submitted an immediate offer. The very next day, I signed an exclusive contract with the real estate agent for selling my property and buying the one at the village. I felt high on the idea of this new horizon and shared my plans with my friends and my other neighbour. This neighbour, who was experienced in the industry, warned me off having an exclusive contract. She didn't think it was a good idea or even necessary.

A very close girlfriend suggested I cancel the exclusive contract, slow down and do my due diligence before rushing in. She felt I might be playing out my pattern of escaping into new horizons rather than staying grounded and present. I contacted the real estate agent immediately and he agreed to cancel the exclusive contract. I slowed down and started to do my research.

As I contemplated selling my home, I realised that I needed to settle the dispute with my neighbour. This would make my home a more attractive proposition for a buyer, particularly in regard to a having stable body corporate situation behind it.

During this time, I was eating breakfast on my back veranda and saw a large kookaburra sitting on a tree branch in my yard, quite close to where I was seated. As I watched and appreciated the bird, I felt strongly it was a sign. Soon after, I was at a dinner party with close friends and was sharing the news about my house adventure and mentioned the kookaburra *sign*. One of my friends searched online for the meaning of kookaburra as a totem and we discovered it represented social behaviours, group efforts, beauty and happiness and also ending old patterns and turning hurt into happiness. My friend suggested that the kookaburra may be a sign for sorting out the dispute with my neighbour, especially as the bird had been in a tree near our mutual fence line.

The conflict with my neighbour had escalated and become very upsetting and frustrating. It culminated in an all-out text war between us, in which we cleared grievances that had built up over several years. As a result, I felt freed up. Within the ensuing month, she had paid her arrears. We had a subsequent body corporate meeting and were able to set new ground rules and arrangements for maintaining the mutually owned property.

Preparing to sell my home had motivated me to complete some long-awaited house updates. I had new downlights installed in the living room and kitchen, new modern venetian blinds set in the windows, arranged for updated smoke detectors and had my air conditioning fixed. At the same time, more creative ideas started to flow on how I could improve the value of my home.

I noticed I was feeling more settled and happier in my current home now that my neighbour issues had resolved. I found myself quite satisfied with my home renovations and was enjoying my new space.

My interest in the village property had waned. It sold to another buyer and, though somewhat disappointed, I realised I wanted to stay where I was for now.

I found myself renewed and happy in my current home."

This woman was able to discover where the flow of her desire was ultimately taking her – to have a more fulfilling and happy home situation.

Her story is a perfect example of being initially driven by a life pattern rather than intuition. In this case, the desire/pattern was to move to new horizons when feeling bogged down. However, by slowing down, staying present, doing some research, accepting feedback from trusted friends and following the signs, she was able to make adjustments along the way. These included clearing up some old relationship hurts and continuing to take action when feeling motivated (house renovations). Together, these actions led her to discover what she truly desired – to be happy in her home with a sense of renewal.

As a postscript to this story, two years down the track, this woman eventually sold her house following a massive property price boom in which her profits increased by a further $200,000. This enabled her to be totally mortgage free, fulfilling one of her original desires, and she has settled into a delightful new property overlooking a river. She also discovered the person who eventually purchased the deceased estate property she had been interested in, had needed to spend significant money on maintenance repairs to that home.

Another important insight from this story is that sometimes your intuition will give you a sense of direction, or vision toward your future, way ahead of time. In this story, the desire to move and be mortgage free was two years in the making. In this case, some elements needed to unfold and synchronicities had to fall into place before the best timing for the manifestation of this vision could occur.

Be sovereign to yourself

By building relationship with your intuition - via trial and correction in small-safe-steps - you will develop an internal validation process enabling you to access your inner wisdom, discern the truth within your life, and become sovereign to yourself.

Your intuition will naturally deliver your personal truth to you. Sometimes you will be guided to choices that take you along your own path, despite the opinions or even judgements of others. No matter what is presented to you, with a well-developed inner knowing, you can run it past your own personal integrity system and discern if it is true and right for you.

What has integrity got to do with intuition? The more you align with integrity, the more your inner pathways of truth become open and available.

Author's note on integrity

"I have found over the years that the more I focus on personal integrity and making choices from a space of integrity, the more information is naturally entrusted to me. I will simply be confided with the truth, or the underlying truth is revealed to me in some way about situations or people, and this will be despite outward appearances. Being aware of the underlying truth can be very useful in navigating my own personal choices. Usually, my intuition has been telling me that something is not quite right, and then I find out what is going on that is not immediately obvious. It is as if the world is telling me the truth as a reflection of my own integrity."

Samantha - Sovereign Family Decisions

"We have three children whom we decided not to vaccinate. We made this decision based on our gut feelings, assessment of our individual circumstances, and thorough research of the literature for and against. This continues to be a confronting decision as there is so much pressure from the medical community, government, schools and other parents regarding vaccinating children. Our alternate decision was based on the risks we see in vaccination together with the fact that I was carrying a serious systemic infection while pregnant with my children, which may have already put their immune systems under pressure.

To this day, I still feel strongly that this is the right decision for our family, despite the pressure around us to the contrary. We have instead supplemented our children with plant-derived nutritional supplements to strengthen their immune system and also use homeopathic remedies. As it turned out, a bout of whooping cough went through the children's school, triggered by a recently vaccinated child. The recently vaccinated child could stay at school, but our whole family was excluded from day-care and required to have prophylactic antibiotics. One of our children contracted whooping cough and responded well to treatment. In general, our children, now 10, 8 and 7 years old, appear equally, if not more, resilient than their peers when it comes to the regular infections inevitable throughout childhood. Sometimes you just have to trust yourself despite the very strong opinions and even societal agreement on certain subjects. It's a very personal decision."

If another person delivers a concept to you from their own belief about something, you can reflect and feel out if it seems true to you. This is being sovereign unto yourself. If you know someone is trying to influence your opinion or choice, check inside and explore what feels right for you and choose from that place. You may or may not agree with what they suggest, or with the popular opinion on certain topics.

Importantly, this includes common opinion about other people. Be aware not to simply align with the agreement field (group opinion) about someone else. Be willing to choose your own truth based on your personal knowing and/or intuition about that person. What is your gut telling you is true for you? This may be in agreeance with others, or it may not.

On the other hand - don't get stuck in being right

On the other extreme, sometimes people can become so stuck in being right about something, they ignore the opinion of their trusted inner circle of friends. If you have friends you trust, who you know have their own developed sense of self, and they are suggesting you consider your choices about something, it can pay to reference their opinion in your decision-making process.

Alternatively, if you find you are unsure whether you are on track with your choices, you can ask for guidance on the matter. See 'Calling upon the truth' in the Practical Steps section of this chapter.

In this following story, you will see that by taking into account the input of a trusted friend, this woman was able to come to the truth of her situation.

Kerrie - Returning Home Early

"I was touring New Zealand with a close friend on a long planned and much dreamt about holiday, when the Covid lockdown escalated. Five days into our two-week holiday, we received the news from our government to, "Come home now." This was not welcome news to me as I was immersed in the joy and reverie of my holiday and the stunning nature of New Zealand. At the time we received this directive, life was flowing just fine, supplies were abundant and there was no sense of panic. I wanted to stay and continue our holiday. However, my travel partner, who I deeply respect, was immediately on high alert and wanted to research the facts. I felt initially resistant to the panic, but as I contemplated, I knew I should respect her sense of alertness, and researching was common sense. When we did investigate the escalating situation, it was obvious things were more serious than I had wanted to believe.

As I had often experienced clarity when in nature, I knew our planned afternoon walk in the local mountains would help me tune in to my intuition on the matter. Deep in the experience of that walk through the mountain forest, it became very clear to me we should return home as soon as possible and afterward made appropriate arrangements to fly back. This was followed by 14 days in home quarantine under Australian government Covid rules. The rest is history – New Zealand went into full lockdown three days after we departed, and all unnecessary travel within the country was halted. All tourism venues closed down and not long after, no international flights were provided. It all progressed incredibly quickly, the pace of which was completely unforeseen.

A week after my return, Australia required all returning citizens to be in 14 days quarantine under army guard in a hotel. I was very grateful my intuition spoke to me with such clarity once I tuned in."

Balance is the key to trusting yourself and your choices, and in referencing the opinions of others, particularly when your intuition may be clouded by desire.

Practical Steps for
Distinctions on the Truth

If you are feeling unclear about your intuition:

1. **Call upon the truth**: you can use intention to call upon the truth. Say out loud across the situation:
   - "If I am in fantasy about this situation, let that be shown to me."
   - "If this choice is not for my highest good, let that be known to me."
   - "I intend to know the truth in this situation and what is for my highest good."
   - "I relax and let go into my higher good on this matter."
   - "I ask for guidance as to that which is for my highest good."

   Keep your eye out for signs and feedback in your world that stand out to you and offer clearer direction.

   Remember, you can ask for signs, or ask your intuition to repeat if you are unclear.

2. **Seek support** via a practitioner, coaching or bodywork to assist you in clarifying any underlying patterns that might be influencing your choices.

   Some actions that will assist to release limiting mind-body-emotional patterns:
   - Intent – use your intention to change the pattern.
   - Talk it through with a friend.
   - Seek support or coaching from a practitioner.
   - Receive energy healing/bodywork from a healer.
   - Take flower essences and/or homeopathic remedies via a practitioner.

3. **Do some journaling:** Write down how you are feeling and reflect on what comes out on paper.

*Deepening your relationship with nature
is a powerful way of connecting with your
intuition, which, in its essence,
is the voice of your own true nature.*

9.
Your Relationship with Earth and Nature

Connecting with the Earth is paramount to experiencing deep intuition. Deepening your relationship with nature is a powerful way of connecting with your intuition, which, in its essence, is the voice of your own true nature.

You are intimately connected to the Earth, sometimes called Mother or Gaia. There are energy grids around and within the planet that connect with your personal energy field, and these grids influence your awareness. The magnetic grid of the Earth is well known for its effects on human consciousness. Indigenous cultures around the world understand their soul connection to the Earth. They experience an intimate cultural alignment with the land and nature and hold a deep honour and respect for that relationship.

In the channelled works of *Kryon,* through Lee Carroll, it is revealed that there are several energy grids which lie upon, around, and through the Earth.[17] These grids have an influence on your soul evolution and your ability to experience a more expanded consciousness. Profound information about the grids, your relationship to them, and the Earth in general, can be found in the book 'The Gaia Effect' by Monika Muranyi.[18]

The bottom line is that your connection with Earth is intrinsic and exists to support your soul's evolution. Regarding intuitive development, the deeper your *conscious* connection with Earth, the more in flow you will be with the essence of truth within you. There is a deep bond that exists with Gaia, which can produce a grounded sense of connection with your Self and allow you to tune into how you truly feel or point you toward your best choices. This connection offers you a clarity that you may not otherwise experience. So, you are certain of choices and/or direction in life and this clarity comes as a felt knowing in your body. The awareness of your bond with Gaia can be enhanced by your intent, loving appreciation, and connecting consciously with *her*.

Feelings and emotions move at Earth's pace - they are slower to emerge than thoughts. We can have multiple thoughts in a microsecond, but emotions generally take longer to come forward and make themselves known to us. By giving yourself some nurturance and slowing down through connecting with nature, you can gain insight into what you are feeling, embrace more inner peace and tune in to your innate knowing.

The Earth's vibration can assist you in slowing down and calming your personal vibration, and in so doing, allowing you to be present with yourself in a deeper, more profound way. When you connect with your Self, you connect with your inner knowing.

Being in nature also helps clear out our physical/emotional/ mental/spiritual cobwebs. This clarity can save time and make decisions easier and more obvious. It also brings joy, and for that reason alone, it is a positive activity to include in your life. Remember, joy brings passion, which enhances and opens the communication channels of your intuition.

Nature is also full of intuitive reflection. You can ponder on aspects of nature and they will offer you insights to life's questions.

Natasha - Being in Nature Brings Clarity

"I had previously visited Australia but found it difficult to establish work and had returned home to Canada. Two years later, a man I met on my first trip had reconnected, and I decided to go back to Australia to explore the relationship. I was very keen to secure a job and establish a long-term stay this time.

My career history was in beauty therapy and massage, so I decided to have my nails done at a local salon to see how beauty services were being provided in Australia. At random, I chose a nearby beauty spa and booked an appointment. As it unfolded, the owner of the salon was on duty and would be doing my nails. From discussions with her about my work situation during my nail treatment, she offered me a trial situation as a massage therapist at her salon.

She loved my work and continued to provide me with shifts. At the same time, I was also doing beachside massage treatments for a local resort, which I was greatly enjoying.

Within a few months, the manager of the beauty salon resigned, and the owner offered me the position. Initially, I didn't want the role because I was happily settled into my routine of massaging on the beach as a second income. However, I decided to meditate on her offer and took some time sitting on the beach in contemplation of what was best for me.

Later that day, just ten minutes before the owner phoned to ask my decision, I changed my mind - I just knew I needed to accept the job.

Three years later, I am still managing the salon and feel in the right place. I have focused on marketing and good customer service, and the business has grown significantly since I have been there. Also, as a result, I have been able to stay in Australia, get married and settle in the area."

In this story, we see how connecting with nature (sitting on the beach contemplating what was best) brought through clarity of decision for her work choices and supported her desire to establish stability and explore her relationship.

Julia - A Clear Message from Gaia

"A friend of mine had been considering the prospect of giving away her cat. She loved the cat dearly, but it had been unwell and seemed unsettled in her new unit. My friend thought giving her away was the only possible solution to the situation. A discussion followed where I suggested being open to other solutions that didn't necessarily involve the loss of her cat.

After our conversation, we went for a walk on a nearby beach and were happily exploring the array of lovely multi-coloured pebbles that had washed up on the shoreline. My friend placed her favourite thongs down on the sand, so she was hands free for fossicking amongst the pebbles. Whilst exploring, a big wave suddenly washed through the pebbles, and when we looked around, her thongs were gone! Where did they go? It only took moments to realise the thongs had been washed out to sea in the wave. As we realised what had happened, another wave washed up the shoreline and delivered both thongs onto the sand right at her feet in a way she could step straight into them! We simultaneously burst out laughing at the play of nature.

We both noticed the *sign* from nature immediately – a message of what was momentarily feared to be lost was immediately delivered right to her feet. A message of trust in solutions being delivered at the very least. In the end, it unfolded that the cat recovered with some homeopathic and veterinary care, and she was able to keep her much loved moggy."

Gaia will speak to you and give you a sign, message or reassurance like this if you are tuned in to her. You may remember a mother's story earlier in this book where a bird's presence would give her a sign about the needs of her daughter: "… I have had many occasions where a bird would fly into my view or make itself known to me in some way, and this became my reminder to take her out into nature."

Linda – A Rainbow Message

"My mother had passed away, so I travelled interstate with my father to arrange for Mum's ashes to be buried according to her wishes, and to share in a family memorial and luncheon. The memorial was very much a family reunion, with lots of open-hearted conversations as we celebrated Mum's life. Afterward, my father and I returned to the 10th floor, sea-side apartment where we were staying.

That afternoon had brought some light rain, and as we stood

on the apartment veranda overlooking the sea, we noticed a double rainbow forming on the beach in the distance. As we watched, the rainbow developed a glorious full double arch across the sky and onto the ocean. It then started to move slowly toward us along the beach from approximately a kilometre away. Eventually one end of the rainbow grounded within the intersection of the street immediately below us and just hung there for a while. It was an extraordinary moment, and play of nature, in which I was certain it was a sign from Gaia, reflecting the loving experience of the celebration of Mum. I felt reassured, peaceful and happy."

Flower essences and intuitive atunement

Intuition is a result of vibrational alignment with communication from your Higher Knowing to your conscious awareness. Utilising vibrational remedies from certain flowers is a method by which you can align with the energies of Gaia to assist with intuitive flow.

Some flower essences are highly beneficial to help tune in to this communication, recognise the messages, and have the courage to take action. There are many ranges of flower essences throughout the world. The information here is about the Australian Bush Flower Essences developed and researched by Ian White, a 5th generation Australian herbalist.[19]

Several of these wonderful bush flower essences can be used as tools for enhancing and *hearing* your intuition, for grounding and decision-making. Here are some recommendations:

Bush Fuchsia: This is *the* primary flower essence for enhancing intuition. It assists in being in touch with, and trusting in, your intuition. It can be taken as a single essence and could also be taken in a combination essence, such as 'Meditation Essence', 'Creative Essence' or 'Calm & Clear Essence'- these combinations contain Bush Fuchsia plus other essences for being present, creative flow, grounding and centring.

Other individual essences that can help with intuitive flow are:

Angelsword: Assists with clearer communication with your Higher Self.

Turkey Bush: Assists inspired creativity to flow.

Once in touch with your intuition and its communication, the next step is to decide what action, if any, you are going to take to back it up. Essences that can support with decision-making are:

Jacaranda: Assists in making choices, especially if you are hesitating in fear of making the wrong decision.

Paw Paw: Assists in connecting with your Higher Self to make decisions and solve problems, particularly where there is a choice to be made between two or more things.

As discussed in this chapter, being grounded and connected to the Earth and nature can greatly enhance your intuitive connection:

Red Lily: Supports being focused and living in the present. Supports being grounded and practical in your day-to-day life, while at the same time feeling connected to the spiritual realms.

Sundew: This works with grounding, centring, and focusing on the details, which also assists in being decisive. If you are procrastinating, it can be helpful in taking action and being decisive.

Also covered in the book, has been the importance of slowing down and relaxing, to assist being in-tune with how you are feeling and what you really want. Therefore, anything that supports you in winding-down, calming and relaxing can assist with intuitive connection. If you know you need to slow down, be more inward and still, the combination essence 'Calm & Clear' would be beneficial. It contains Bush Fuchsia, Paw Paw and Jacaranda, which all support intuition and decision-making, plus contain essences for centring, relaxing and calming.

This is a very basic overview of how the Australian Bush Flower Essences can support your intuitive development and knowing. For a deeper understanding, you could refer to the book 'Bush Flower Healing', by Ian White[20] Interestingly, Ian has brought forward the understanding of the Australian Bush Flower essences and their healing influences through meditation, dreams and his intuition.

All Australian Bush Flower Essences and support materials are available at www.ausflowers.com.au [21]

During the course of my Intuitive Mastery Program, I recommend participants take a combination of these flower essences to enhance their experience of developing and trusting their intuition.

Your personal connection with Gaia

You can embrace the interrelationship you have with Earth and further deepen your intuitive awareness. Your personal energy field is intimately connected with Gaia. Within this connection lies the access points to expanding your awareness and knowing things beyond your immediate reality. This access can awaken via deepening the connection with your personal energy system. In Chapter 8, we discussed the mind-body-emotional patterning held within your energy body. Here we are covering how you can work with your energy system to gain receptivity to your Greater Knowing. A great place to start is by consciously connecting with your chakras or energy centres.

Chakra awareness and multi-dimensional communication

Within your energy body are chakras, which are spinning energy centres (or vortices of light) that serve as gateways for the flow of consciousness and life force into your physical body. There are many chakras throughout your body, but the largest are the seven main chakras that align your spine and head. They run from front to back like funnels meeting in the centre at their smallest point. These funnels act as energy communication freeways through which you can receive and transmit information, including intuitive communication. In relation to your physical body, the openness and flow of energy through your chakras is thought to determine your state of health and balance.

In addition to the chakras, there are several layers of *energy bodies* or energy fields which radiate outward in an elliptical shape around your physical body. These energy fields are layered much like an onion, and each has different vibrational qualities reflecting various aspects of your make-up.

The layers are:

1. Etheric body (Closest to the physical body)
2. Emotional body
3. Mental body
4. Astral body

5-7 are spiritual bodies.

8-12 extend the farthest from the physical body and relate to your soul and your connection with Divine Source.

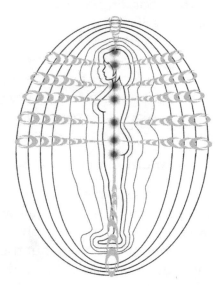

Figure 2. Seven main chakras and seven layers of our energy system

Rather than being separated, these layers interface with each other, including with your physical body. Your energy system also incorporates the enormous electromagnetic field of your heart, as mentioned in Chapter 4, which encompasses every cell in your body and extends out several feet in all directions from your heart centre.[22] All this is part of a massive consciousness field that is known to extend up to 26 feet beyond your physical body and is contained within the human Merkabah – a *vehicle* of light energy containing sacred geometry in which your soul rides. You can search online using the phrase *Merkabah with torus field* to view pictures. Via your extended energy field, you are in touch with and have the capacity to *read* information that is immediately around you. This explains why when someone walks into a room you can, at times, intuitively tell how they are feeling before they say anything.

The spinning vortices of the chakras interchange through these energy layers and pass information inward and outward. Your perception is via these chakras, and each chakra is particularly receptive to the different *voices* of your intuition. The bottom line is - you are a very grand and sophisticated energy being, the essence of which is love, and have the potential to access many levels of awareness. Your communication capacity goes way beyond your immediate surroundings. It expands to multi-dimensional communication available through your greater energy system, which is known as *multi-dimensional consciousness* – an awareness that knows things beyond time and space. This is a known area of quantum physics that is still being explored and understood. There are far more complex and thorough explanations of the human energy system and chakras elsewhere.[23] The purpose of this brief explanation is to provide you with a basic awareness that you have access to an energy system around and within you that provides you with intuitive information via energetic communication pathways.

Multi-dimensional communication via your greater energy system translates to sensations, feelings, senses, sounds, images and sometimes smells. These are experienced in your physical body, which I have called the Voices of Your Intuition. A brief summary is provided below, though please see Chapter 6 for more in-depth information.

Physical sensations: goose bumps; chills; gut feelings; hunches.

Hearing: words; sentences; songs or parts of songs; hearing *messages*; words jumping off the page; another's words that *stand out in bold* to you.

Vision: receiving a picture or vision in your mind's eye - symbolic or metaphoric; dreams.

Love: as an open-hearted connection with others in which you can sense or know things about them; love as guidance – "I knew in my heart."

Feelings/Emotions: fear; anger/resistance; excitement/passion/desire.

Knowing: simply knowing things or knowing the truth; inspired or creative ideas.

Our intuitive perception via our greater energy system can give us a much bigger picture than is immediately obvious.

Knowing all this, it is easy to understand that any kind of chakra alignment meditation can assist in receiving clearer intuitive communication. Chakra meditations are also supportive to emotional and physical wellbeing.

There's a broad variety of chakra and energy system meditations, ranging from simple to very complex, with the purpose of activating various aspects of energy and awareness. A simple Chakra Alignment exercise is outlined in the Practical Steps section of this chapter. This exercise has been designed for you to gently build a conscious relationship with your chakras so that the communication you are receiving becomes clearer.

As we establish more balance and centredness within ourselves through meditation and conscious connection with our greater energy system, our intuitive wisdom, which emanates from our Greater Self, becomes more readily accessible.

Practical Steps for Connecting with Nature

Connecting with nature

Anything that connects you with nature will be excellent for your health and your intuition. Simply going for a walk somewhere inspirational is a beneficial thing to do. The deeper you explore your connection with the Earth, the better.

Just as love is the connecting factor with your intuition, love is the power by which you consciously connect with Gaia.

Simply be in loving appreciation of Gaia

You could choose to be aware on a daily basis of the abundant provision of Gaia in your life and give heartfelt thanks. For example, for the land you live on, the food on your table, any nature you enjoy around you, the companion animals you have with you. This alone can build a conscious connection and flow of goodwill to you.

The four core elements of nature are: earth, water, fire, and air. You can use any of these elements to connect with nature.

Important note: As you practice the activities below, use your conscious awareness to gently focus and connect with the Earth element at hand. It is this combination of your gentle conscious intent to connect and your loving appreciation, together with the actual interaction with the Earth element, that establishes a deeper connection.

Earth

Lie on the earth – Take some time to lie on the ground somewhere. If you use a towel, blanket or sheet beneath you, it is best to choose a natural fibre such as cotton or wool, as this will easily transmit the vibration of the Earth. You can align your chakras with the energy of the Earth by lying flat on the ground.

Firstly, lie on your front or back, close your eyes and consciously connect with the Earth. Focus your mind on connecting your chakras with the earth and send love and appreciation to her. Breathe into the idea of connecting your chakras to the pace of Earth's vibration. You can visualise this if you like. Breathe and relax. You will feel your body relax and centre. You can choose to flip over and lie on the alternate side, doing the same.[24]

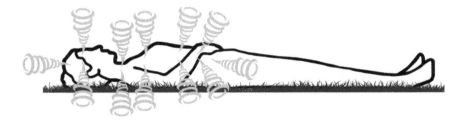

Figure 1. Aligning your chakras with the energy of Earth

Walk on the earth barefoot: Walking, standing or sitting with your bare feet on the earth for 15 to 20 minutes can do wonders for grounding and centring your energy system.

Read a book sitting on the Earth or under a tree: Take time to sit under a tree to read. If you sit with your buttocks touching the ground near where the tree enters the earth, there is a strong grounding force in that location.

Gardening: Is a great way to connect with nature.

Grounding meditation: If you are unable to be outside, you can take yourself there in your mind's eye with visualisation.

Make yourself comfortable, close your eyes, and visualise a chord of light moving down from the base of your spine deep into the earth and connecting you to a name plate that says, "*Your name* – grounded in present time." Breathe and relax into that connection. See the energy flowing down that chord of light and connecting you to the earth. Breathe and relax into that grounding force. Be in appreciation of this connection.

Crystals: Crystals are known to enhance awareness. You can utilise holding crystals or gazing into them to amplify insight and healing.

Water

Spend time in water: Immersing your body in water and relaxing is a great way to connect with yourself and your inner knowing. Swimming in the ocean or a stream is a wonderful method of clearing your energy field and mind. Floating and soaking in a warm bath can bring you into the present and more in tune with how you feel. A nice addition could be to add your favourite essential oils or minerals such as Epsom Salts to the bath.

Simply being in a shower with the water casting down and around you can set the stage for flashes of insight, answers to questions, or deeper knowing to come forward in your awareness.

Be in appreciation of the release and relaxation the water offers you.

You could use this affirmation:

"I welcome the Divine water element, Spirit of Water, to cleanse my body spirit. I thank the Earth for accepting this and disposing of it in safe and appropriate ways."

Fire

Sit by an open fire: Relaxing by, or gazing into, an open fire indoors or outdoors is another meditative action that your intuition will respond to.

You could also choose to gaze meditatively with soft eyes at the flame of a candle. Breathe and relax.

Connection with community, celebration and laughter also ignites the fire element within – you could combine these activities around a fire.

Air

Breathing: Practice deep breathing, yogic breathing, breathing meditation, taking a deep breath or doing *Breathwork*.[25] These are all ways you can use your breath to relax, let go, and become present with yourself and your inner knowing.

Your breath is the gentle breeze that opens the doorway to your subconscious and allows you to be in touch with your truth deep within you. You could start with one sigh and then allow your breathing to become slower and deeper into your soft belly.

Exercise: Any form of exercise can be beneficial for assisting you in extending your breath and becoming more present with yourself. Various forms of exercise are considered to be quite meditative, such as swimming, rowing, walking or running.

As you move, it causes your energy to circulate and your breath to increase, which can increase your clarity of mind. It also assists in shifting the focus away from your mind and into your body as you move physically and put your attention to the exercise at hand. This can allow for intuitive flow to happen at times. Many people receive clarity on issues they have been contemplating, or new inspiration, during their exercise program.

Smudging: Burning sage, Palo Santo or other herbs and woods is a wonderful way you can experience the cleansing benefits of the air element. The passing of smoke through the energy body is used by many indigenous peoples as part of traditional ceremonies to clear away the old and welcome in the new.

You can burn some incense to lighten the space around you or in your home. Choose scents that make you feel good and give you a sigh of relief to have them in the air.

Wind: Going for a walk in nature on a windy day can certainly be invigorating and clear the energy around you and within your mind.

Nature's reflection

Nature is full of reflection. The following exercise can provide insight into your own psyche and how you are truly feeling about things. It is an effective way of becoming present with yourself and gaining a view to any action you could take to be self-supportive.

Pick any object in nature that takes your attention (don't overthink it) and then go through this written exercise below, using it as a reflection of your current inner nature.

Let go of any judgement of what comes into your mind. It will be unique for everyone and reflective of where you are personally in that moment.

You can also use this exercise to gain insight into the symbols within your dreams. Simply replace the object in nature with the symbol in your dream.

For example, if the object in nature you choose is a tree:

As this .... e.g., *"tree"* ....
What I am feeling is .... e.g., *"tall and on my own"* ....
What I need most is .... e.g., *"to connect with others"* ....

Together, this culminates in, "As this tree, I am feeling tall and standing out on my own and what I need is to connect with others."

For example, the object in nature is a red bush:

As this .... e.g., *"red bush"* ....
What I am feeling is .... e.g., *"driving passion"* ....
What I need most is .... e.g. *"to stay focused but take it slow and steady. Slow and steady wins the race."* ....

This example generates the insight, "As this red bush, I am feeling driving passion and I need to stay focused, but take it steady also."

This exercise is reproduced with permission from Diamond and River Jameson, creators of Total Integration Institute: livingfreedom.info [26]

Simple Chakra Alignment

This simple Chakra Alignment exercise is designed to assist you in gently building a conscious relationship with your chakras so that the intuitive communication you are receiving becomes clear and more available.

When you think of the chakra colours, the colours of the rainbow can give you a good reference. If you are guided to use a different colour, then trust that.

Sit quietly where you won't be disturbed, with your eyes closed.

Take a deep breath and relax.

Welcome your Guides, Angels and the beings of light that support you in your work, journey, purpose and joy here. ASK them to wrap their loving energy around you.

Now visualise a column of gentle silver-white light casting down around and through your body and flowing into the earth beneath you.

Then see a chord of golden light flowing down through the centre of that column of light, gently entering through the top of your head, flowing down your spinal cord and down into the Earth. See that chord connecting you to a golden name plate deep in the Earth that says "... (*your name*) ... *grounded in present time*."

Bring your awareness to your **base** or **root chakra** at the base of your spine. This is the area of the first chakra and the colour is **red**. Visualise a ball of red light gently spinning in that chakra. Simply be gently present with that chakra, with the intention of connecting with, centring and grounding in that chakra. Breathe and relax and send love to the chakra.

Move your attention to a place approximately in the centre of your pelvic area just below your navel. This is the area of the **sacral chakra,** and the colour is **orange**. Visualise a ball of orange light gently spinning in your second chakra. Simply be gently present with that chakra, with the intention of connecting with, centring and grounding in that chakra. Breathe and relax and send love to the chakra.

Bring your awareness to your **solar plexus**, which sits just below where the rib cage separates and above your navel. The colour is **sunflower yellow**. Visualise a ball of yellow light gently spinning in your solar plexus. Simply be gently present with that chakra with the intention of connecting with, centring and grounding in that chakra. Breathe and relax and send love to the chakra.

Move your attention to your **heart,** behind your breast-bone. The heart chakra is green and may have a pink glow. Visualise a ball of **green** light gently spinning in your heart chakra. Simply be gently present with that chakra, with the intention of connecting with, centring and grounding in that chakra. Breathe and relax and centre in the love in your heart.

Bring your awareness to your **throat** chakra located at the base of the throat, where it meets your collar bone. The colour is **deep lapis blue**. Visualise a ball of deep lapis blue light gently spinning in your throat chakra. Simply be gently present with that chakra with the intention of connecting with, centring and grounding in that chakra. Breathe and relax and send love to the chakra.

Move your awareness to the centre of your brow where the **third eye** chakra is located. It centres on the pineal gland in the mid brain and is the seat of intuition. The colour is **indigo** (deep purple-blue). Visualise a ball of indigo light gently spinning in this chakra. Simply be gently present with that chakra, with the intention of connecting with, centring and grounding in that chakra and receiving through your Higher Knowing. Breathe and relax.

And finally, to the centre of the top of your head where the **crown chakra** resides. The colour is **violet** or **opalescent.** Visualise a ball of violet or opalescent light gently spinning in this chakra. Simply be gently present with that chakra, with the intention of connecting with, centring and grounding in that chakra.

Breathe and relax and send love to the chakra.

Now see the golden chord gently connecting all your chakras – connecting you with heaven and with Earth.

Relax for a while, gently breathe, and be in a state of love and appreciation for yourself.

Then, gently bring your awareness back to your body in the room and your contact with the ground.

When ready, gently open your eyes.

*Perhaps the most profound truth
about the intuitive process is
you are absolutely never alone.
Spiritual support and guidance
abound around you.*

10.
Spiritual Assistance

There are many methods of deepening the relationship with your intuition. The following have been outlined so far, and methods to further develop these are described in the Practical Steps section at the completion of each chapter:

- Using your intention for intuitive connection.
- Embracing the guidance from your feelings and emotions.
- Utilising practices that develop deeper self-love and self-worth.
- Living with compassion and integrity.
- Utilising small-safe-steps in trusting and following your intuition.
- Including your logic and education to back-up your intuitive guidance.
- Slowing down and listening deeply.
- Pushing on the door of your inspirations.
- Building a relationship with the unique repertoire of your intuitive voice.
- Connecting with the special tonality of your intuitive messages.
- Looking out for, and following, the signs and synchronicities as they occur.
- Being in a state of release and allowing the messages to guide you to clarity.
- Calling upon the truth, asking some universal questions and utilising repeated messages for guidance.
- Connecting with Earth and nature.
- Understanding your intuitive awareness will evolve and deepen over time.

Your light worker support team

Perhaps the most profound truth about the intuitive process is that you are absolutely never alone. Spiritual support and guidance abound around you.

We each have many helpers in the spiritual realm. There is an abundance of *beings of light* or *light workers* in other vibrational realms who support your spiritual life and can offer assistance with your inner guidance system. Some people resonate with the concept of Angels, though it might not appeal or be of interest to you. Some people relate more to the idea of the *Goddess* or *Guides* or other helpers. Regardless of *who* you relate to, they are all from the same benevolent Source. It is important to understand that these helpers are not directors giving orders, but rather have a connection with your Higher Self and hold an overview of your life. They can offer guidance for your highest good, but ultimately, you remain sovereign and responsible for your own choices.

Only you can know the best choices for yourself, and you do that via your intuition. Intuition emanates from your innate self, which knows everything about you and is connected to your Higher Self. Your Higher Self lives in a harmonic relationship with your *light worker support team* and ultimately with Divine Source.

Love is the connecting factor

Your heart is the connection point with your Higher Guidance and the same is true with your light worker support team. You can build a conscious relationship with your spiritual support team through invitation and imagination, focusing on your heart as the connection point. Imagine your Angels/Guides around you and send love from your heart to them. Then imagine them sending their love to you. Imagine receiving a sense of their loving presence. This process creates a conscious bonding and an awareness of their loving support. It opens the pathways of communication so that you can move towards a daily living relationship with them and experience their love and benevolent guidance.

Your light worker support team is always there with you, whether you are aware of it or not. It is not necessary for you to *see* your Angels or Guides for them to hear and assist you. Nor is it a requirement that you know their names. Your heartfelt intent to communicate through asking for their assistance is enough to make the connection. In time, you may identify your light worker support team more clearly, however, this is not needed for their loving care to be delivered to you.

You have to ask

You can ask them to give you a sign they are there for you, and you can ask them for guidance. You can also ask them for assistance with healing in any aspect of your life. Of course, they hear any request in your mind. Yet it is best to speak it out loud for the same reasons as any intent - it assists your mind to focus on what you want and brings your intent into physical form via the vibration of your spoken word.

Your light worker helpers will communicate with you in whichever way you will best recognise via your intuitive repertoire; signs, synchronicities, visions, feelings etc. Rather than this information coming purely from your inner knowing, it is communicated from your Angelic helpers via the pathway of your intuition. You may build your own repertoire of Angelic communication. You can even receive *signs* letting you know that they are there for you – these will be unique to you. Some examples could be; finding white feathers along your pathway; feeling a wave of their love move through you (sometimes called a *love wash*); catching a glimpse of an Angel in your mind's eye; receiving *answers* to the prayers you have communicated to them.

It is important to understand that these Light Beings are not more powerful or intelligent than you. In fact, in some ways, they are reflections of your Greater Self. However, they do have a helpful overview of your life, the potential available to you, and what you are aiming to achieve at a soul level.

They are dedicated to assisting you on your journey and are just waiting to serve at your request. Even so, it is an absolute rule that *you have to ask* for their assistance – this is Spiritual Law. They cannot step in without your request because you are living in a world of free choice and must give conscious intent to connect. A friend of mine once joked that we have to ask our Angels to get off the gin rummy table. Meaning that they are sitting by, patiently waiting for you to ask them to get to work. What a tragedy to have a whole lifetime go by without ever having asked for their loving assistance, when you have had an entire support team on standby just waiting for your request. There are tremendous positive outcomes that can occur in your life if you engage them by asking for their help.

Rhianna - Found It!

"I was employed as a disability support worker and amongst my clients was a gentleman with dementia. Twice a week I would visit and support Daniel in walking outdoors to keep him active and mitigate his decline.

Daniel was completely obsessed with his watch. It appeared very old, and I believe he had owned it most of his life. When he woke in the morning, he reached for the watch, and before we left the house, he insisted having the watch on.

One day I arrived at the house and his daughter told me he had lost his watch. They had been looking for it all day and she asked me to spend some time doing another search before we departed for our walk.

Daniel and I explored the entire house but couldn't find it. I said to him, "Don't worry. We will ask the Angels to find it." I told him we should ask aloud and he laughed at my suggestion which, as an 83 year-old, was completely out of his world of experience.

However, there we were together, asking out loud for the Angels to help us find his watch.

After this, we were leaving the house for our walk. As I opened the front door, I noticed, over to the right of the entrance, a rag dropped off a clothes rack which was placed there. I walked over to put the rag back on the clothes rail, and low and behold, when I lifted the rag, the watch was right under it on the ground! It had fallen in a very unusual place by a pot plant at the edge of the outside wall of the house.

My whole body vibrated with goose bumps at the discovery. Daniel was ecstatic to have his watch returned. He looked at me, pursed his lips while lifting his shoulders and said, "Mmm... okay, seems it worked." We both laughed out loud, and I felt incredibly satisfied with his little acknowledgement of the Angels' assistance. "Thank you, Angels!"

Asking for Direction

If you are seeking clarity in a life situation, you can ask for help and guidance from your Angels.

Alice - He Was Framed

"I was attracted to a man who lived around the corner from my home and could feel the attraction was mutual.

Being a bit of a dreamer, I am careful not to waste my time and energy in fantasising about possible relationships. Because of this, I asked the *Universe* to give me a sign as to whether it was beneficial for me to keep thinking about him – which of course I was – a lot!

Following this, we continued to bump into each other in the street, and on one of these occasions he asked for my phone number. I felt very excited about the prospect of him being in touch, however he never called or texted. I noticed I was making excuses in my head for why he had not contacted me.

Every time we met by chance in the street, I felt excited, yet after the conversation I would experience a gut feeling that he wasn't good for me. In addition, he was continually putting me on hold about getting together.

Around this time, my cousin came to visit and asked the inevitable, "Who are you seeing?" I filled her in on my *bump-into* friend. Subsequently we met him while out walking, and afterward she boldly told me she didn't have a good feeling about him.

I decided to sit down, meditate, and directly ask my Angels to give me a sign about this man. I requested they show me in a *picture* whether he was right for me. (*I receive picture visions in my mind's eye and have grown to trust them as reliable guidance*). I completely let go and didn't expect anything in particular.

The next day my cousin and I were walking around the corner from my apartment. There was an art gallery across the street, and they were throwing away old picture frames. My cousin enjoys painting and I like to draw, and that week were doing some art creation together. We walked across the road to inspect the frames. As I lifted a frame to measure it in my arms, I heard someone laughing behind me. I turned around and, through the frame held in my arms, I saw the man outside his house where he was having a party. He was drunk, hugging two women, and I was witnessing this all through the view of the picture frame I was holding!

The message was clear, and following this witnessing I let the idea of him go completely. Subsequently, he moved and I haven't seen him again."

This story above is a wonderful example of directly asking for guidance and receiving it. The literal message of a picture framed right in front of her eyes was an unmistakable, yet funny sign in response to her request for clarity. On occasion, you will see the light side of how a message is delivered in your life. This is known as *cosmic humour.*

The following story is an extension of one previously shared in Chapter 7, which concerned a woman seeking to gain clarity on her desire to move from the city to a regional living experience. In this version she explains aspects of her story which relate to the Angelic guidance she requested, and received:

"I was participating in Diana's Intuitive Mastery program, in which she was teaching about our connection with our Angels and suggested to invite my Angels to give me guidance.

My routine was to go for regular walks in the local forest prior to my workdays. On my previous early morning ventures amongst the trees, I would stop and face the sun, and meditate. One time I experienced a vision where I had a sense of the sky drawing me upward to a beautiful light upon a path. As I approached, I recognised a figure of light who then held my hand. I felt deeply safe and cared for. Now, with more understanding, I suspected this had been a connection with my Angels and felt they could help me with clarity on my desire to move.

The morning after participating in the course, I went for my walk and consciously asked for clear direction from my Angels. Amazingly, I discovered several feathers on the path which I had never previously seen. I counted them and there were nine. This felt significant and a sign of affirmation of my desire. I *knew* that morning we were on the right path for pursuing moving.

From that point onward, my knowing became stronger and stronger. I continued to talk with my Angels and Guides and thanked them for being there. Each day I felt more encouragement from them, that moving was the correct choice for me. I noticed a sense of being guided out of my comfort zone and yet knowing I had to follow it.

The following weekend I spoke with an intuitive friend and told her about the nine feathers. She told me that the number nine represented *completion,* "You are completing something in your life," she said. Indeed, I felt at the end of a chapter in my life.

I always believed I would know when it was the right time to relocate, and this is exactly how I felt - the time was right.

Another highly intuitive friend told my partner she had envisioned a price we would receive for the sale of our home. The amount was way above our expectations, however our real estate agent confirmed the potential value of our home was in that range. This validated that our desired change of lifestyle was within our financial reach. We wrote the exact dollar figure our friend had visioned onto hand-written notes and placed them around our house. When we sold, this was the precise amount we received for our home!

I regularly asked for guidance throughout the process. Everything started to flow and fall into place without effort. My partner and I began researching real estate and found the property of our dreams – four acres of land with a large lake, established gardens, fruit trees, a hen house and stunning country surrounds. A friend who lived nearby was able to do a walk through with the real estate agent, and we made our decision immediately. Bidding for purchase resulted in our favour, and we were absolutely elated. It was all systems go for our move to the country."

Beyond this woman's direct request for guidance, this story is rich with signs (feathers on her path, validation of property value supporting the move), synchronicities (friends interpreting signs, having visions and being available to support), and flow (everything falling into place in perfect timing), fully validating her chosen direction.

Angelic intervention

Rarely will your helpers give directional guidance. If they do, it is usually in response to a life-threatening situation or related to a choice that is important for your soul direction. The message may have a sense of not coming from within you. However, you are perceiving it through intuitive reception, such as having visions or hearing voices or feeling stopped in your tracks. You still have the choice to act or not and sometimes your response will be immediate.

In addition, there may be occasions where you experience unusual delays in the course of your life, or the unfolding of a plan. Later in retrospect you see those hold-ups resulted in better timing for you.

Donna - In the Nick of Time

"I had been travelling home on a bus and was in the process of disembarking at my stop.

As I was exiting the bus, I attempted to pay using my phone credit card system, but it didn't work. I tried another time and still, it did not work. Finally, on the third go the credit card payment processed. All this delayed my departure from the bus.

As I stepped off the bus, a young boy on a mountain bike came speeding right toward me, almost on top of me at this stage. He saw me, slammed on his brakes, then passed right across the front of my body. He was in shock, and I was too. If my exit had not been delayed, he most likely would have hit and seriously injured me.

I pursue a very active relationship with my Angels, inviting their love and support in my life on a regular basis. I believe my Angels had a hand in my safety that day."

Gentle Guidance

Usually, guidance and support will be along the lines of giving you signs for direction or a gentle nudge in some way that appears to say, "This might be a choice worth considering," or "Look over here," or "Wrong way – go back." You always have free choice as to what action you might take with that information.

It is your soul connection to these beings of light and Divine Source that creates a synergistic energy for the synchronicities to show up in your life. You can ask these helpers to assist with setting up the synchronicities on your life journey that will guide you to good choices.

Having a living relationship with your Angels or Guides, or whoever it is that you resonate with the most, will bring you peace and joy and greater ease. It is just like having extended family taking care of you.

You can thereby utilise this connection as additional support to enhance your intuition to a whole new level of fulfilment and purpose.

In the following story, a woman has beautifully integrated her intuition and Angelic connection into her work.

June – Ceremonies with Deeper Purpose

"I have been a Marriage and Funeral Celebrant for over a decade and love my work!

When planning a funeral service, I believe the passed over loved one guides me regarding the content of their ceremony. I always consult the family as to whether the beloved had any spiritual beliefs and receive an impression of their essence. This gives me an idea of how the person felt about Spirit and what I might include in their ceremony.

When delivering the service, I always sense my Angels with me. Whenever I feel the need for extra courage and strength during a ceremony, I directly ask for their presence. A beautiful calmness comes over me and a knowing they are right there with me, as if they are communicating, "We've got you." In addition, while delivering the ceremony, I will often feel the passed over loved one standing with me.

One day, a friend of mine expressed being in awe of my emotional strength in delivering funeral services, and I related it was because of my Angelic helpers. That very night, I woke from my sleep, and experienced a vision of a beautiful, radiant Angel floating and shimmering in brown and gold hues above me. I asked myself if I was dreaming and reached out to touch my husband, who was breathing and sleeping gently next to me.

In my mind, I heard the Angel say, "This is what we look like." The Angelic outline faded and was replaced by a beautiful swatch of colour in radiant gold, and I heard the words, "And this is our colour." I felt incredibly grateful for this gift of confirmation of their loving presence in my life.

Following this, a friend who runs a local magazine, asked me to give an interview about my experience as a Celebrant. I was delighted to do this but asked for guidance as to whether I might open up in the interview and share how I welcome Angels to assist my funeral services and my weddings.

I chose a quiet time while lying down to ask my Angels whether to include this aspect of my ceremonies in the interview. I had placed my phone on silent and when I arose, I noticed a message had arrived from a Facebook friend. She had written a piece of music about the transition of life to death and shared it with me.

While listening to the song, I felt myself go into a very deep meditation where I was completely immersed in the experience. I found the words and music purely uplifting, like a hymn, and felt amongst the Angels in a way that brought me to tears. During the meditation, it dawned on me this experience was a confirmation to share my story of the Angels' connection with my work.

When the owner of the magazine took my photograph for the article, I discussed the idea with her. Incredibly she said, "Oh that's perfect, I would love you to speak about the Angels. We are living in a time where we should share these kinds of stories. It will encourage others." This was further affirmation to me.

As it turned out, the Journalist who interviewed me was a spiritually minded woman. She was also enthusiastic about the inclusion of the spiritual aspect of my ceremonies. The published article was a beautiful reflection of my work, including my connection with the Angels, and their support to the service and families dealing with the transition of a loved one."

There is no judgement

Your support team never judges you. If you are perceiving judgement, it is not from your Higher Self or your light worker support team. They exist in a different realm of awareness to you, where there is no view of right and wrong. Their consciousness is one of benevolence, compassion, love and kindness. Any guidance is toward your most beneficial choices, not right or wrong choices.

As with the process of following your intuition, you can always correct and choose again if you find you have gone down a pathway of resistance. You will benefit most when you hold a patient, forgiving, and compassionate attitude toward yourself. This then frees you up to shift and change and navigate to better choices. Instead of fixating on negative or regretful thoughts or reprimanding yourself for your actions, a loving and compassionate approach will release you to focus on positive aspects and opportunities and to notice signs and synchronicities.

Invocation

You can invoke a clearer connection with your Higher Self and your light worker support team to assist and guide you. You can never be disconnected from your Divine Source, but you can have your back turned, thinking or pretending it doesn't exist. Through invocation, you can turn front-on and receive the benefit of a clear connection and communication with the part of you that is all-knowing and thereby enhance your intuitive awareness.

There are some sample invocations at the end of this chapter, but the following story is just one example of other ways in which that connection may occur.

Diana - Meeting My Angels

"I had been experiencing substantial psychic disturbance in my life and sought help from a healer. She gave me a meditation to do every day where I visualised myself in a citadel of light and affirmed out loud my connection to a Higher Light and my sovereignty over my thoughts, actions and emotions. Several days into this daily practice, seemingly all of a sudden, my awareness expanded, and I was conscious of being surrounded by beings of light (very bright) who were wholly loving. It was as if they were simply showing me they were there. I just *knew* they were Angels.

This was a whole-body experience, and I felt safe, loved and deeply peaceful. I wanted to remain in that state forever. The experience lasted for about half an hour, and when I finally emerged from this state, I knew I could return to it with practise of prayer and intent. I had never given much thought to Angels prior to this event, nor had I read anything about them, so afterwards I visited a local esoteric bookshop to find more information. There began a passionate study to understand more about Angels and their purpose in my life. I have pursued an understanding and connection ever since and experience a deeply rewarding relationship with the beings of light that support my work and my journey through life."

Resting back in the arms of your Angels

There may be times when you have no idea about your direction in life. You could feel lost, confused or maybe even hopeless about your circumstances. Perhaps you have no sense of the connection with your intuition or clarity of inner knowing at all.

At these times, it can be part of the intuitive process to consciously imagine resting back into the arms of your Angels. This is a state of letting go, where you can imagine their support around you and imagine leaning back into their support, love and guidance.

It involves trusting they will be there for you and hold a clear overview of your life. Believe that you will be given guidance in perfect timing, but for now there is nothing to do but rest back, trust and be loved.

From this state of peace, your intuition will emerge and guide you once again when the timing is right. This might require some patience, as the shift to peace or clarity may not be immediate.

Note: Some people might prefer to imagine resting back in the arms of God, but many will find the Angels more relatable for them. This process is inherently individual, and either way it will work, as long as you focus on believing a Divine Source is there for you and backing you up.

Practical Steps for Connecting with Spiritual Assistance

Invoking a Higher Power

We all have a Higher Self and are connected to a greater source of Divine Energy. In multi-dimensional reality these co-exist.

From our human 3D perspective, we can experience:

1. Our direct connection with our Higher Self and Divine Source.
2. The loving support of the beings of light dedicated to assisting us in our life journey.

Ultimately, they are one, and you are one with it.

You can invoke a clearer connection with Divine Source and welcome your light worker support team to assist and guide you on a daily basis.

Sample invocations

Connecting is simple – just ask with pure intent.

Here are some starting examples. Remember, you can use whatever words you relate to best. Just start somewhere and allow it to evolve until the words sit right with you.

Invocation to your Divine Source:

"I welcome a clear connection and communication with the Divine Source within me. Move through me and make my way clear. I intend right action to move through me for my highest good. I welcome you as a living experience in my life."

Invocation to Beings of Light:

"I welcome the living presence of my Guides, Angels, and beings of light that support me in my work and my journey here. I welcome your love, support and guidance in my life. Let me know your loving presence. Walk with me on my journey. Bring your grace to my intentions so they manifest in support of my highest good. Let the signs be clear for me. Let me know the way."

Connect with your LOVE. The invocation process includes a physical aspect, whereby you connect energetically from your heart and send love to your Angels/Guides. Allow yourself to feel the love that is there for you, or imagine it being returned. Imagine the Angels holding you in a loving embrace, sending a wash of love through you. Intend your pathways of connection to be open and clear. Simply be with the feeling of this loving experience for a while.

Resting back in the arms of your Angels

This visualisation can be done at any time to build a relationship with your Angels. It is particularly wonderful to do if you are feeling stressed or lost in your life.

Close your eyes and imagine your Angels and Guides around you. Take a moment to imagine their loving energy surrounding you. Breathe into the knowing they are there for you. Imagine relaxing into their support and presence – lie back, resting into a soft energy that suspends you. Invite their loving presence to support you. Breathe and relax. Consciously welcome their love and guidance. Choose to be in a state of trust that this is given to you. Relax. Breathe.

Let go of expectation of any specific outcomes.

Speak with your Angels daily. This will build the conscious awareness of your connection. Remember, your Angels and Guides are your close loving friends who want to be in communication with you.

Ask for a sign that your Angels are with you. Invite your Angels to give you evidence of their loving presence. These signs will be unique to you and having meaning for you. Trust your intuition when these indications show up in your everyday life.

Ask for guidance. If there is something in your life you would like clarity about, ask your Angels out loud for clearer direction. You can ask your Angels to set up the synchronicities that will guide your way. Then release it and be open to receiving the signs and synchronicities in the course of your life.

Ask to feel their loving presence. You can build familiarity with the energy of your Angels. It may feel like a peaceful, calm warmth that flows through you. Perhaps you experience goose bumps, or as a deeper experience you may feel a wave of their love moving through you. Trust yourself when you feel an indication of their loving presence.

Choose to hold the belief you are never alone. Your Angels are always present and loving you whether you are aware of them or not.

*Intuition is the wheelhouse that drives your
evolution. It is predestined to guide you into a
deeper connection that will further support
your expansion and wellbeing
– as if in an ever-expanding circle.*

11.
Living an Intuitive Life

Ultimately, the development of your intuition becomes intuitive itself. As you develop the connection, you may start to notice your intuition guiding you to choices or activities that lead to an even more expanded awareness of your inner knowing. Intuition is the wheelhouse that drives your evolution. It is predestined to guide you into a deeper and greater connection that will further support your expansion and wellbeing – as if in an ever-expanding circle. It all starts though, with your intention to connect.

Deep intuition is not an overnight sensation. It is similar to the development of a long-term relationship that deepens and strengthens over time. It is refined through life experience and the building of trust. It is nurtured through self-love and the letting go of judgement of your knowing and inspirations.

Be light with the process of exploring your intuition. Sometimes you will be on track with your choices and sometimes you won't. Be willing to learn, trust that the Universe will back you, be humble and make a correction if needed.

Develop patience and openness with the unfolding of your inner guidance. There is far more involved within the Universal process than we will ever fathom. If you accept the concept that you are one with everything, this means you are in relationship with everything, and part of a much larger picture that is continuously evolving and changing. The timing and direction of that evolution are being influenced by the individual choices of many. Your *desired* timing may not be the best timing for the perfect unfolding of your life within the greater Universal plan. Be patient and develop the wisdom to wait for the signs and synchronicities to act and allow time for things to develop. Choose to believe that benevolent good is always being delivered to you.

My heartfelt desire is that you align with this benevolent flow and learn to trust your deep inner wisdom which is leading you along a path of increased fulfilment and sense of purpose. May your intuition become part of your daily living experience and enhance every aspect of your life, including where you are led to make a difference.

My prayer is that the tools and stories I have shared provide useful guidance and reference points for developing an intimate relationship with your unique intuitive style.

A most enjoyable path

It is rewarding for me to hear stories of what unfolds when people trust their inner knowing and find themselves in the receipt of their greater good. I would be delighted to know of your experiences as you use these tools to follow your intuition. You can connect with me to share your stories, ask questions, or enquire about personal consultations via the links at the end of the book.

Remember to have fun with it! The overwhelming message from Source Energy is that we are meant to enjoy ourselves and follow what makes us happy. I am convinced our intuition will lead us on the most enjoyable, fulfilling and rewarding life path.

So, enjoy your journey!

Wishing you fulfilment along the path.

With love and gratitude,

Diana

Recommended Resources

Brennan, Barbara Ann. *"Hands of Light,"* Bantam UK. 1ˢᵗ Edition 1994 www.barbarabrennan.com

Carrol, Lee. *"The Kryon Series volumes 1 to 13,"* The Kryon Writings Inc. USA. 1993 to 2018. The other works of Lee Carroll can be found at www.menus.kryon.com

Hicks, Esther and Gerry. The works of Abraham-Hicks can be found at www.abraham-hicks.com

Jameson, Diamond and River. Total Integration Institute, www.livingfreedom.info

Losier, Michael. *"Law of Attraction,"* Grand Central Publishing. New York, USA. 2010 www.michaellosier.com

Muranyi, Monika. *"The Gaia Effect,"* Ariane Editions. QC, Canada. 2014 www.monikamuranyi.com

Muranyi, Monika and Dr Amber Wolf. *"The Women of Lemuria,"* Ariane Editions. QC, Canada. 2018 www.monikamuranyi.com

White, Ian. *"Australian Bush Flower Healing,"* Bantam Books. Australia. 1999 www.ausflowers.com.au

Highly Recommended Movie about Intuition

Bennett, Bill. *"PGS – Intuition is Your Personal Guidance System,"* Producers Bill Bennett and Jennifer Cluff. Australia. 2021 https://www.pgsthemovie.com/watch-now/

Endnotes

1   Carroll, Lee. "The Kryon Series volumes 1 to 13" The Kryon Writings Inc. USA. 1993 to 2018

2   Jameson, D. Jameson, R. Total Integration Institute, www.livingfreedom.info

3   Hicks, Esther. The works of Abraham-Hicks can be found at
    www.abraham-hicks.com

4   Muranyi, Monika. The works of Monika Muranyi can be found at
    www.monikamuranyi.com

5   Carrol, Lee. "The Kryon Series volumes 1 to 13," The Kryon Writings Inc. USA. 1993 to 2018.
    The other works of Lee Carroll can be found at
    www.menus.kryon.com

6   Transcendental Meditation (TM) www.tm.org

7   Transcendental Meditation (TM), "Seven Levels of Consciousness"
    www.tm.org

8   Foundation for Inner Peace. "A Course in Miracles" (ACIM). Penguin Books, England. 1975

9   Orr, Leonard. Rebirthing Breathwork International,
    www.rebirthingbreathwork.com

10 Ray, Sondra. Loving Relationships Training (LRT), Sondra Ray Programs and Seminars

11 I first learned about the trilogy of our heart, mind and innate knowing - and the power
    of achieving confluence between them - from the channellings of Kryon through Lee
    Carrol.
    Carrol, Lee. "The Kryon Series volumes 1 to 13," The Kryon Writings Inc. USA. 1993 to 2018.
    The other works of Lee Carroll can be found at www.menus.kryon.com

12 Schwartz, Stephen Lawrence. "Defying Gravity," From the Album "Wicked" Original
    Broadway Cast Recording 2003

13 McCraty Ph.D, Rollin. "Science of the Heart" HeartMath Institute. USA 2015 https://www.
    heartmath.org/research/science-of-the-heart/energetic-communication/

14 National Geographic Society (1996-2021)

15 I first heard this lovely analogy, for the concept of exploring our inspirations, expressed in
    the Kryon teachings. You can find the works of Kryon at
    www.menus.kryon.com

16 Michael Losier has written an excellent book explaining various methods for identifying
    and attracting the conditions and circumstances that you want in life. Losier, Michael.
    "Law of Attraction," Grand Central Publishing. New York, USA. 2010   www.michaellosier.
    com

17 Carroll, Lee. "The Kryon Series volumes 1 to 13" The Kryon Writings Inc. USA. 1993 to 2018

18 Muranyi, Monika, "The Gaia Effect," Ariane Books, Qc Canada 2013

19 White, Ian. Founder of Australian Bush Flower Essences.
    www.ausflowers.com.au

20 White, Ian. "Bush Flower Healing," Bantam. Australia. 1999

21 Australian Bush Flower Essences (ABFE) www.ausflowers.com.au

22 McCraty Ph.D, Rollin. "Science of the Heart,"" HeartMath Institute. USA. 2015 https://www.
    heartmath.org/research/science-of-the-heart/energetic-communication/

23 Barbara Ann Brennan has produced an extensive body of work covering the human
    light body which I highly recommend. Her work can be found at www.barbarabrennan.
    com

24 I first learned a practice of earth connection similar to this through the work of
    Diamond and River Jameson. Jameson, D. Jameson, R. Total Integration Institute, www.
    livingfreedom.info

25 Orr, Leonard. Rebirthing Breathwork International, www.rebirthingbreathwork.com

26 Jameson, D. Jameson, R. Total Integration Institute, www.livingfreedom.info

About The Author

Diana Hunter

Master Intuitive, Spiritual Healer, inspired author and gifted speaker, Diana Hunter, has over 40 years' experience in the Healing Arts. Diana's spiritual awakening was initiated at a meditation retreat at the age of 21. What followed was a passionate exploration of personal development, spiritual healing practices, body work, and a deep understanding of relationship dynamics and emotional healing. In addition, her initial career in allied health transformed to a lifelong study in natural health which she also applies within her healing modalities.

Diana's intuitive development was triggered by a deep emotional healing experience during the 1980s. She had the insight of how she could enhance the connection with her inner wisdom and access guidance for a purposeful life. Diana utilised many processes to deepen her intuition and evolved as a Master Intuitive Healer and Medical Intuitive. She developed the gift to intuit the patterning people are holding in their mind, body, emotions and spiritual life, and offer guidance on how to bring that into balance and harmony. This includes the capacity to intuit the underlying patterning of dis-ease.

Diana has pursued a relationship with her intuition as guiding force in her life. Her book *An Intuitive Life*, delivers practical guidance on the secrets and rewards of developing intuitive mastery, in a way that anyone can have access to the magic and power of their inner knowing.

Since 1992, Diana has also actively participated in women's spiritual and emotional healing groups and believes in the power of women supporting each other to their highest potential. She enjoys the retreat of nature on the Sunshine Coast, seeing private healing clients, and teaching her Intuitive Mastery courses both online and in groups. Her courses empower people to develop the bridge to their Higher Knowing and enjoy the path of *an intuitive life*.

Learn more about Diana's work or contact her at:

Email: diana@dianahunter.com.au

Website: www.dianahunter.com.au

Instagram: dianahunter_healer

Facebook: You can find me on Facebook: diana.hunter.946

CPSIA information can be obtained
at www.ICGtesting.com
Printed in the USA
BVHW062153090323
660106BV00016B/183